The U.S. Congress

A Simulation for Students

Second Edition

Lauren Bell

Randolph-Macon College

Australia • Brazil • Canada • Mexico • Singapore • United Kingdom • United States

CENGAGE

The U.S. Congress: A Simulation for Students,
2nd Edition
Lauren Bell

SVP, Higher Education Product Management: Erin Joyner

VP, Product Management, Learning Experiences: Thais Alencar

Product Director: Laura Ross

Product Manager: Lauren Gerrish

Product Assistant: Martina Umunna

Content Manager: Manoj Kumar, Lumina Datamatics Limited

Digital Delivery Quality Partner: Liz Newitt

Product Marketing Manager: Valerie Hartman

IP Analyst: Deanna Ettinger

IP Project Manager: Nick Barrows

Production Service: Lumina Datamatics Limited

Designer: Sarah Cole

Cover Image Source: Fotosearch/Gettyimages

For product information and technology assistance,
contact us at **Cengage Customer & Sales Support, 1-800-354-9706
or support.cengage.com.**

For permission to use material from this text or product,
submit all requests online at **www.copyright.com.**

Library of Congress Control Number: 2021922917

ISBN: 978-0-357-66026-3

Cengage
200 Pier 4 Boulevard
Boston, MA 02210
USA

Cengage is a leading provider of customized learning solutions with employees residing in nearly 40 different countries and sales in more than 125 countries around the world. Find your local representative at **www.cengage.com**.

To learn more about Cengage platforms and services, register or access your online learning solution, or purchase materials for your course, visit **www.cengage.com**.

Printed at CLDPC, USA, 11-21

For my students, who bring me immeasurable joy;
for my family, which instilled in me the need to always keep learning;
and for Jim, whose love and support makes everything possible.

Contents

A Note to Instructors

Although the simulation described in Chapter Three prescribes a particular set and sequence of activities, this simulation is intended for individual instructors to adapt and change to work well within their particular courses. In the companion materials for this simulation, I offer suggestions about how to adapt this simulation to a variety of class settings and how to accomplish a variety of instructional objectives. For example, I describe several optional exercises that can be used—or not—depending on such factors as class size, achievement level, student interest, and your own desire. In addition, although I encourage students to be active in choosing their own leaders, selecting the members that they want to portray, and framing the content of their legislation, instructors may prefer to handpick the students to play leadership roles or to exercise more control over the flow of the simulation. Finally, the timing of the simulation is also flexible. The activities can be spread out over the course of a semester, compressed into a few weeks at the end of a course, or used individually to illustrate or emphasize a particular point. The companion materials provide aids to make this simulation run smoothly for both the students and for instructors, no matter how the instructor decides to integrate it into their classes.

Instructors should feel free to adapt and change assignments, to prioritize assignments differently, and to decide how best to use the particular strengths and interests of the students in their classes. Instructors should also make any changes that will improve the flow of the simulation or that will encourage students to participate. In my own courses, I have required some of these activities to be done outside of class time. I have also required students to contact one another outside of class using email, discussion boards in our learning management system, and via other forms of communication, such as group texting or chatting. I have found that students in my courses who participate in this simulation are more often engaged in the class, more likely to do the assigned reading (because they know that it helps them to portray their members and to participate more fully), and are more likely to report high levels of learning. In making this simulation available to other instructors, it is my hope that they, too, will experience these same benefits.

Instructor Resources

Additional instructor resources for this product are available online. Instructor assets include an Instructor's Manual and PowerPoint® slides. Sign up or sign in at www.cengage.com to search for and access this product and its online resources.

Preface

Although I first started doing simulations with students in the fall of 1996, my first experience with a simulation was as a senior in high school. My high school government teacher, Nial Davis, taught us to think about government by "doing" government. He used a simulation called Community Land Use Game (CLUG), which had been developed in the 1960s by Professor Alan Feldt at Columbia University. Even today, more than three decades later, I vividly remember role-playing a city council member as we dealt with community development problems, natural disasters, and unscrupulous colleagues in our quest to improve our simulated town. My experience playing CLUG with my classmates inspired in me a lifelong passion for the study of politics and government.

It was with this experience in mind that, as a teaching assistant for Professor Gary Copeland at the University of Oklahoma during the fall semester of the 1996–97 academic year, I proposed a simulation of the U.S. Congress. Professor Copeland graciously gave me the freedom to design such a simulation, which I did, and which became the foundation of this simulation.

Many people have assisted me over the years in the development of the simulation. Chief among those are the students that I have the privilege to teach each day. Discussions with students at the University of Oklahoma, Bucknell University, and Randolph-Macon College have led me to identify new and different techniques that can be used to help students understand the way the Congress works. In the preface to the first edition of this simulation, I thanked several former students by name. I have now been teaching long enough that the list of students whose thoughtful feedback has helped me to refine this project is too lengthy to reproduce here. But, each time I use the simulation with one of my classes, I identify new and better ways to use it to reinforce the other course material—largely because the students make suggestions that improve the experience—and I am grateful to all my former students who have helped me to craft a more thorough, engaging learning activity.

Much of the material in this simulation is gathered from participant observation as a member of the 1997–98 class of the American Political Science Association's Congressional Fellowship Program, and as a U.S. Supreme Court Fellow working in the Office of Legislative Affairs at the U.S. Sentencing Commission in 2006–2007. These opportunities immersed me in the ways in which Congress works—and the challenges confronting the institution—and I am grateful for the support of those involved with both programs for the chance to engage in participant observation of some of the most important processes of governing. Yet Congress has also changed significantly since I worked in these roles, and so I am also enormously indebted to dear friends and former students who work in or adjacent to Congress, who have made sure that I am up to speed on the ways in which the institution continues to evolve. I especially need to recognize Lesli Gooch, Troy Lyons, and Tyler Cianciotti for their counsel and support in this respect.

I owe my current colleagues in the political science department at Randolph-Macon College a tremendous debt for their support even as I teach less and less in the department. I am deeply appreciative that professors Brian Turner, Tom Badey, Rich Meagher, and Elliott Fullmer continue to support my work. Elliott's counsel and collaboration on simulation activities is especially noteworthy, and I am grateful to him. I am grateful as well to my colleagues in the Randolph-Macon College Provost's Office, including Alisa Rosenthal, Susan Parker, Bill Franz, Sandi Robison, Diana Lewis, Debra Marklin, Margaret Ann King, and Denise Thompson, who over the years have supported me to meet the needs of my students above all other responsibilities in the office.

Acknowledgements

As every author knows, even single-authored texts are group endeavors. This simulation physically would not exist if not for the dedication of several people involved in its production. Our work was greatly aided by the Politics editor at Cengage, Emily Hickey, who provided detailed feedback on each of the revised chapters and gave valuable insight on how to best approach thorny topics. Others such as Manoj Kumar, Lauren Gerrish, Sheila Moran, and Barbara Long helped keep the project moving and bring it to a successful conclusion. Finally, I deeply appreciate the comments of the following reviewers who helped me to sharpen my focus and refine this simulation:

Augustine Hammond Augusta University

Jarrod Kelly North Carolina Wesleyan College

Young Kim North Carolina Wesleyan College

Matthew Platt Morehouse College

Eleanor N Powell University of Wisconsin-Madison

Greg Rabb Jamestown Community College

Ryan Voris Abraham Baldwin Agricultural College

———— 1 ————

An Introduction to the Simulation

- Understand the purpose and goals of this simulation.

- Describe how the Constitution structures the legislative branch of government.

- Identify the ways in which Congress has changed over time.

One purpose of any course is to immerse students in its subject matter. There is no better way to immerse students of political science in the subject matter of the U.S. Congress than to have them simulate the experiences of its members and engage themselves in the functioning of the body. For this reason, I developed this simulation of the workings of the U.S. Congress.

Through this process, you will simulate the U.S. Congress at work. Although the simulation focuses primarily on the House of Representatives, additional optional exercises are included that allow for the class or group to examine the U.S. Senate as well. This simulation focuses on the House for several reasons. First, the House operates under stricter rules of procedure and is more easily simulated than the Senate, which operates under more flexible rules. Second, and related, the House vests its leaders with greater institutional power, which allows you and your classmates more hands-on control of the simulation itself. Finally, House membership is far more diverse than the Senate membership— there are far more female-identifying people and persons of color in the House than there are in the Senate. Thus, although the demographic profile of neither body mirrors the population, the House somewhat more accurately reflects the diversity of the American public. This provides you with greater opportunities to select members of Congress who mesh well with your own interests, policy preferences, and personal background or to select a member to portray that is very different from you, allowing you to gain a new perspective on the issues and concerns that are important to others.

This simulation is meant to be an enjoyable way to assist you in grasping the intricate workings of politics, law, procedure, and legislation in the U.S. Congress. In order for this simulation to work, however, you and your fellow students in the course will have to do your part. Your instructor will act as the Speaker of the House and (if your class is including a Senate component) the presiding officer of the Senate. As the Speaker or presiding officer, it will be your instructor's job to be focused and organized, to present you with the information you need or with the guidance necessary to find it on your own, and to ensure that the simulation runs smoothly.

Ideally, your instructor will also take precautions to see that the composition of your simulated House of Representatives closely mirrors the demographics, partisanship, geographic distribution, urban/rural distribution, and committee structures of the actual House. In that way, the simulation is structured so that each student has the opportunity to obtain a maximum of hands-on experiences with the legislative process. At the same time, if the simulation is to be effective, *every* student must participate in *every* simulation activity; remember, once the simulation begins, you have a responsibility not only to your simulated Speaker and fellow House members but to your "constituents," your country, and your conscience as well. In short, your job is to complete each simulation task to your best possible ability.

Many of the activities in this simulation focus on what we might call the "textbook" Congress. That is, the emphasis is on how members of the U.S. House engage in their roles as *legislators* and **representatives**. The activities you'll participate in include many of the important aspects of representatives' work on Capitol Hill—crafting legislation, defending it in committee and on the floor, working with co-partisans, and communicating with your constituents. But the simulation omits other activities that consume significant time and energy for House members, such as fundraising, media appearances, and coordination with interest groups and **senators**. Many of these activities are critical to their efforts to be reelected, which is why members spend time both on legislative activities and representation and on reelection activities. As you participate in this simulation, compare your work in your simulated Congress to what you see and hear in the media about the actual Congress, and consider the ways that real congressional work is both similar to and different from what you are doing in this simulation.

Simulation Goals

You should come to understand several things through your participation in this simulation. They include:

1. The complexity of making legislation.
2. The ways in which **members of Congress** work separately and together to make the laws.
3. The role of politics in how Congress works.
4. The difficulty members of Congress have in balancing their various commitments to their constituents, their party, their committees, and their own consciences.
5. The difficulty of creating new laws and the impact of partisanship on the lawmaking process.
6. The connection between elections and lawmaking.

Before describing how the simulation works, it is useful to make note of several important points about the history and evolution of the U.S. Congress. Students,

Representative. A member of the U.S. Congress serving in the House of Representative and representing a congressional district within a state.

Senator. A member of the United States Congress serving in the U.S. Senate, representing a state.

Member of Congress. When used throughout the text, this term refers to members of both the U.S. House and U.S. Senate.

just like the members of Congress they will role-play, need to have certain basic information about the Congress in order to fulfill their responsibilities.

The Congress Then and Now

After this section, you will be able to:

■ Understand the design of the Congress in the Constitution.

■ Identify the ways in which Congress has changed over time.

The U.S. Congress emerged from several important compromises. In 1787, when delegates from the thirteen newly independent states gathered in Philadelphia for the Constitutional Convention, one of the only things they agreed on was that the Articles of Confederation had not worked. The delegates were divided, however, over whether to create a unicameral (one-chamber) or bicameral (two-chamber) legislative branch. Without debate, but by a vote of seven to three, the delegates opted for a bicameral Congress.[1] They were also divided over the questions of apportionment of seats between large and small states and representation of noncitizens (enslaved people and Native Americans). In what has come to be known as the **Great Compromise**, the delegates at the Convention agreed that one chamber, the House of Representatives, would be apportioned based on population, and the other, the Senate, would be equally apportioned with two senators per state. This compromise resolved the tensions between large and small states at the Convention because it permitted large states a greater number of representatives in the House, but gave the smaller states a representational advantage in the Senate. The consequences of this decision reverberate today because small states are now overrepresented in the Senate by a substantial margin as compared with larger states.[2]

In addition to the Great Compromise, the **Three-Fifths Compromise** was also crucial to the creation of the Congress. The delegates agreed that enslaved people would be counted as three-fifths of a whole person for the purpose of representation and taxation. This compromise appeased the Southern states—which had previously threatened to leave the Convention—because they would be able to count the human beings they held in bondage toward their total number of representatives in the Congress. As historian Jan Ellen Lewis has noted, the Three-Fifths Compromise codified a political order that made population the basis of representation, rather than other options such as property ownership or ability to vote.[3] In doing so, Lewis argues that the framers ensured that debates over who should "count" or be permitted to participate in politics would continue across the entirety of American history.

Like the Great Compromise, the Three-Fifths Compromise continues to have consequences for the modern Congress. As civil rights lawyer Janai Nelson explains, the legacy of "disappearing" communities of color resulting from the Three-Fifths Compromise lives on in the processes associated with administering the U.S. Census and apportioning congressional districts.[4] Recent studies have also demonstrated that voters are more likely to indicate that they feel better represented by members of Congress who share their own descriptive characteristics, such as racial background or gender identity.[5]

Great Compromise Agreement made between large and small states at the Constitutional Convention of 1787 to create a bicameral (two-house) national legislature, with seats in the lower house, the House of Representatives, allocated based on a state's population and seats in the upper house, the U.S. Senate, allocated equally, two per state.

Three-Fifths Compromise Agreement made between Northern and Southern states at the Constitutional Convention of 1787 to allow enslaved people held as property within the states to count as three-fifths of a full person for the purposes of taxation and the allocation of seats in the House of Representatives.

The House and Senate were designed to operate differently, in addition to the different apportionment schemes. The House was to be directly elected by the people. Indeed, the House was the only part of the federal government outlined in the Constitution that was to be elected directly and was to be directly accountable to the people. Until passage of the Seventeenth Amendment in 1913, Senators were to be selected by the legislatures of each state. Moreover, the House was given what the framers believed would be a powerful leader, the Speaker of the House, while the Senate would have to be satisfied with a leader who had additional duties as Vice President of the United States.[6] Nonetheless, because of its indirectly-elected membership, its advanced age requirement (30 as compared with 25 for House members), and its smaller size, the Senate was intended by the framers to be the wiser, more temperate of the two chambers.

The early Congresses met in New York City or Philadelphia, until a permanent home was found for the national government in Washington, D.C., in 1800.[7] Construction on the national capital complex took nearly three decades and was interrupted by the War of 1812, during which, in 1814, British soldiers burned to the ground most of the new government buildings in Washington. Members of the early congresses lamented the poor state of the Capitol building and the surrounding areas. In part because of the inadequate facilities, most members of the early House of Representatives served only a single term, and some did not serve even a full two-year term. Other reasons for the high levels of turnover in the early Congresses include the fact that members of Congress—like the American population more generally—held public service in the fledgling government in low esteem.[8]

Despite the high levels of turnover, the early Congresses were remarkably homogenous. The members of both the House and Senate who served during the early part of the nineteenth century were all white and all male identifying people. Nearly all of them were farmers and—because of the demanding nature of farm life—found that the part-time nature of the early Congresses suited them just fine.[9] Moreover, most members of the early Congress were wary of appearing power-hungry, so they were reluctant to introduce or champion legislation. As Young points out, the Congress was "out of sight and at a distance" from the people that it represented.[10] For most people, there was little reason to pay attention to the Congress.

Much has changed. Unlike the farmer-legislators of the early nineteenth century, today members of Congress come from all walks of life. Although many are attorneys or have had previous experience working in government at the state or local level, many others come to the Congress from careers in medicine, nursing, or pharmacy (e.g., Senator Rand Paul, R-KY; Representative Karen Bass, D-CA; Representative Eddie Bernice Johnson, D-TX; Representative Paul Gosar, R-AZ; Representative Cori Bush, D-MO); careers in education (e.g., Senator Jon Tester, D-MT; Representative Virginia Foxx, R-NC; Representative Don Young, R-AK; Representative Jamaal Bowman, D-NY); or careers in business (e.g., Representative Pete Aguilar, D-CA; Senator Marsha Blackburn, R-TN; Representative Barry Loudermilk, R-GA).

It is not surprising that so many members of Congress hail from professional backgrounds; the salary of a member of Congress is $174,000 per year—a rate that has not changed since 2009.[11] While this is still a good salary, it is important to remember that nearly all members of Congress, with the exception of those from districts adjacent to Washington D.C., must maintain two households in two different parts of the country. For this reason, as well as the fact that the costs of running for office are considerable, it is not surprising that so many members of Congress have amassed some amount of personal or family wealth before running for office.

Nevertheless, a few members still come from traditional careers similar to those of members of the early Congresses. For example, Representative Daniel Newhouse and Representative Cathy McMorris-Rodgers, both Republicans from Washington State, note their backgrounds in agriculture. Some members identify the military as their most significant career path, such as Representative Seth Moulton (D-MA) and Representative Dan Crenshaw (R-TX). Other members come from more unusual backgrounds: Representative Don Young, the Republican at-large member from Alaska, boasts "riverboat captain" among the careers he's had. Democratic Representative Kweisi Mfume from Maryland lists "program director for a radio station" in his official congressional biography.[12] In short, members of Congress come from varied backgrounds.

What these members have in common, however, is their interest in serving their communities and their fellow citizens and their ability to connect with people. Unlike members of the early Congresses, who were reluctant officeholders, today's members of Congress often work diligently to stay in office for several consecutive terms. In some congressional elections, incumbency rates exceed 95 percent. Although this is often described as a hunger for power by these members' electoral opponents, most members of Congress sincerely wish to serve their constituents and find that real policy impact is only possible after a period of several years. This is because it takes significant time for members of Congress to develop both policy expertise and procedural expertise, as well as to form interpersonal relationships with other members.

In addition to more varied career paths, today's Congress is much more likely to be populated by **professional politicians**, who make a career out of serving in elected office and who seek to stay in office by running for reelection. Where the members of the early Congresses might have been the only ones willing to stand for election to the office, today a seat in the U.S. Congress is highly coveted by both amateur and professional politicians. This means that each of the 535 people who serve in the Congress today have had to be **electable**, possessing a set of important characteristics, including the ability to run a campaign, raise funds, and persuade the public. These skills help to give constituents confidence in the leadership and policy-making abilities of their member of Congress.

As if running a campaign and winning election were not arduous enough, the transition from "candidate for Congress" to "member of Congress" can also be a difficult one in the modern Congress. Despite a new member orientation session, new members frequently find it difficult to find their way early in their terms. Both the U.S. House and U.S. Senate operate under very specific rules, many of which date back to the First Congress (1789–90). In addition, each chamber has its own norms—informal, often unwritten, rules—that members are expected to abide by. In the Senate, these norms

Professional politician A person who makes a career out of serving in elected office and who seeks to stay in office by running for reelection.

Electability possessing A set of characteristics, including the ability to run a campaign, raise money, and persuade the public, which improves a person's chances of being elected to Congress.

traditionally have included respect for the institution, respect for more senior members, reciprocity, and restrained behavior.[13] Historically, new senators were expected to defer to their elder counterparts, and junior senators who sought too much power too soon were punished through institutional mechanisms designed to keep them in their proper place. In the House, norms have traditionally included allegiance to political party, respect for the rules of the chamber, and respect for the leadership. Recent scholarship has identified several ways in which historical norms of consensus, such as respect for more senior members, have given way in both the House and the Senate to be supplemented or even replaced by norms of conflict.[14]

Although new members attend an orientation session to familiarize themselves with the rules, norms, processes, and procedures, most new members lament that there is little that prepares them for the reality of life in Congress. New members have to attend to ramping up offices both on Capitol Hill and back in their home states. Doing so involves making myriad choices about how to allocate staff members. Members of the House receive a "Member's Representational Allowance" that allows them to hire up to eighteen staff members total (plus up to four more if they meet very specific conditions),[15] but how many people they hire, where they work (at home or on the Hill), and what they do is entirely up to each member. As a result, between the House and the Senate, there are 535 "member enterprises,"[16] representing innumerable approaches to balancing members' policy work, constituency service, and press and social media efforts. How members set up their offices may reflect their priorities; members with large numbers of legislative staffers are likely to be more focused on lawmaking, while members who primarily hire media relations staff are more likely to be focused on building a personal brand.

Once they are established in office, members of Congress find themselves attending countless meetings with their party leaders and co-partisans (party caucuses), with their committees (committee hearings, markups, executive business meetings, etc.), with interest groups, and with constituents. These meetings are in service of their roles as representatives and lawmakers and of their responsibilities to their constituents, their parties, and their country. As Figure 1.1 demonstrates, the daily schedule for most members of Congress is often divided into increments of thirty minutes or less, sometimes from breakfast through dinner. Not only do members have to attend literally hundreds of meetings per week, but they are also responsible for learning something about the thousands of items of legislation that are introduced each year in the U.S. Congress.

Figure 1.1 A Day in the Life of a Member of Congress*

Wednesday, March 6th, 2019

7:30 – 8:00 AM	Member Prayer Group
8:00 – 9:00 AM	Local College and USDA Leadership Breakfast
9:00 – 9:35 AM	GOP Conference
9:35 – 10:05 AM	Radio Interview
10:05 – 11:30 AM	Joint Committee Hearing
11:30 – 12:00 PM	Constituent Meeting
12:00 – 12:30 PM	Lunch: Tuesday Group
12:30 – 1:00 PM	Lunch: Republican Study Committee
1:00 – 1:30 PM	National Association of Letter Carriers
1:15 PM	Votes
1:30 – 2:00 PM	College of Agriculture
2:00 – 2:30 PM	Full Committee Roundtable
2:30 – 3:00 PM	America's Maritime Labor Unions and US Flag Shipping
3:00 – 3:30 PM	National Association of Chain Drug Stores
3:30 – 4:00 PM	College of Agriculture
4:00 – 4:02 PM	Floor Speech
4:05 – 4:30 PM	US Army corps of Engineers
4:30 – 5:00 PM	National Real Estate Investors Association
5:00 – 5:30 PM	Evening Reception
5:30 – 7:00 PM	Evening Reception
7:00 – 8:00 PM	Evening Reception

*Modified from a schedule obtained from a Member of the United States
House of Representatives.

Chapter Summary

In this introductory chapter, we have explored the purposes of this simulation and considered the design of the U.S. Congress in the Constitution. We have also explored some of the ways in which the Congress as an institution has changed—from being a part-time legislature subject to the availability of farmer-members that reluctantly served for short periods of time, to being a full-time legislature made up of professional politicians from varied personal and career backgrounds. Where the early congresses were populated with legislators who were reluctant to exercise the rights and perquisites of office, today's Congress is composed of long-serving politicians trying to promote the public interest while also serving their own desires to be reelected. Members find themselves pulled in multiple, competing directions, with their interests in lawmaking and constituency service frequently in tension with their needs to raise funds for their own reelections and for their parties. All of this takes place within the complicated congressional ecosystem of rules and norms, previously discussed, that constrains their behavior.

The next chapter addresses the nuts and bolts of the legislative process. It is important to have a solid grasp of the way the legislative process works before proceeding to the simulation itself, which is detailed in Chapter 3. Chapter 3 provides instructions for the activities, actions, and processes required to simulate the U.S. Congress. Chapter 4 describes resources available for further study of the U.S. Congress. Finally, the appendices provide examples of actual bills and resolutions, examples of **Dear Colleague letters**, and information about how to obtain a job or internship on Capitol Hill.

> **Dear Colleague letter** Letter written from one member of Congress to other members to discuss a problem, seek support for a legislative proposal, or announce an event. These letters are an important means of communication and information sharing between members and their staffs.

Key Terms

representative 2

senator 2

Member of Congress 2

Great Compromise 3

Three-Fifths Compromise 3

professional politician 5

electability possessing 5

Dear Colleague letters 8

2

The Legislative Process

Learning Objectives

After this chapter, you will be able to:

- Describe the major steps of the legislative process in the House of Representatives.

- Recognize and define important terms related to lawmaking.

- Identify the ways in which the "textbook" Congress has yielded to "unorthodox lawmaking" in the legislative process.

- Describe the ways in which changes to the legislative process have had implications for the types of laws that are passed by Congress.

The preceding chapter investigated a bit of the Congress's history. This chapter turns to providing both an overview and a detailed description of the complex legislative process used by the Congress. It discusses not only the "textbook" steps a proposal must go through in order to become a law but it also explores the ways in which the legislative process in the U.S. Congress today bears little resemblance to the textbook process in Figure 2.1. This chapter also addresses the ways in which actors in the legislative process such as organized interests and party leaders affect policy outcomes and may complicate the legislative decision-making process for rank-and-file members of Congress.

The Textbook Legislative Process

After this section, you will be able to:

- Describe the major steps of the legislative process in the House of Representatives.

- Recognize and define important terms related to lawmaking.

The primary purpose of the U.S. Congress is to make laws, although it also serves other important functions. Indeed, lawmaking is one of Congress's four core functions, and it can be used in the service of at least one of its other functions—representation. (Congress's other functions include oversight of the executive branch and legitimation of the U.S. system of government.) Through the process of making laws, members of Congress engage in a range of activities, including the funding of existing federal government agencies and programs, the creation of new programs and services to serve the needs of the American people, representation of the public's interests, and the staffing of government. Members also use the lawmaking process to enact change in support of their own policy preferences and their constituents' needs.

Lawmaking is carried out through the legislative process, a complicated system of information gathering, legislation writing, debate, and voting. Nearly every textbook written for an introductory American government class or course on the U.S. Congress provides a model of the legislative process. It generally depicts or describes the series of steps that a piece of legislation must go through in order to be enacted into law. These steps, outlined in Figure 2.1, are described in the first part of this chapter. As we will see, however, many of these textbook steps no longer adequately explain what the late Congress scholar Barbara Sinclair called the "unorthodox lawmaking" process that better characterizes Congress's modern legislative procedure.[1]

1. A bill is introduced in the House or in the Senate.

bill   A piece of legislation; requires approval in identical form by both houses of the Congress and must be signed by the President in order to have the effect of law.

public bill   A bill that addresses a general question or whose passage affects the general welfare of the United States.

private bill   A bill that focuses on a specific individual or on a matter that affects a specific individual.

joint resolution   Another type of legislation; like a bill, must be passed in identical form by both houses of Congress and approved by the President, unless the joint resolution is proposing a constitutional amendment. Unlike public bills, joint resolutions are typically used for matters of limited scope.

simple resolution   Used when an item of pending business affects only one house of Congress; needs the approval of only a single house of Congress in order to take effect and is binding only on the house of Congress that passes it.

In the House, legislation is dropped into the "hopper," a box on the side of the Speaker's rostrum. In the Senate, senators introduce legislation by reading it from the floor, although Section 2 of Rule XIV of the Senate provides that such reading "may be by title only, unless the Senate in any case shall otherwise order."[2] Members can introduce several different types of legislation (see Table 2.1). Most legislation gets the title of "**bill**." In order for a bill to become a law, both the House and the Senate must pass it in identical form and the President must approve it. Bills are designated with the prefix "H.R." in the House and "S." in the Senate and can take one of two forms. The first is **public bills**, which are items of legislation that affect the general welfare or address a general question. In contrast, **private bills** are pieces of legislation that focus on individual matters that affect a specific person (e.g., a bill granting diplomatic immunity to a prominent foreign leader). Bills are numbered in the order in which they are introduced in the Congress, with the exception of any numbers that have been reserved by the leadership for "special" legislation or leadership priorities. **Joint resolutions** are essentially the same as bills in that they must be approved in identical form and signed by the President if they are to take effect. The exception to this is joint resolutions that are used to propose constitutional amendments, which are not presented to the President, but instead are sent to state legislatures for ratification. In addition to being used to propose constitutional amendments, joint resolutions are typically reserved for matters of limited scope (e.g., an emergency appropriation of funds); they are frequently used to authorize military action and for proposed constitutional amendments.[3] Joint resolutions are identified by the designation "H. J. Res." in the House of Representatives and "S. J. Res." in the Senate.

In contrast to a bill or a joint resolution, a **simple resolution** is used when the item of legislation is relevant only to the house of Congress in which it was introduced. This type of legislation is not presented to the other chamber for consideration nor is it presented to the President for signature. Examples

Table 2.1 Types of Legislation

Type of Legislation	Abbreviation	Short Description

Bill
 	
   Public Bill
 	
   Private Bill
	H. (House)
	S. (Senate)
		Must be passed in identical form by both chambers and approved by the President.
		
		A public bill addresses a general question or the public welfare.
		
		A private bill focuses on a specific individual or on a matter that applies to a specific individual.

Simple Resolution	H.Res. (House) S.Res. (Senate)	Used when an item of pending business affects only one house of Congress; needs the approval of only a single house of Congress in order to take effect and is binding only on the chamber that passes it.
Joint Resolution	H.J.Res. (House) S.J.Res. (Senate)	Must be passed in identical form by both houses of Congress and approved by the President, unless it is proposing a constitutional amendment. Typically used for matters of limited scope.
Concurrent Resolution	H.Con.Res. (House) S.Con.Res. (Senate)	Must be passed by both houses of Congress but is not sent to the President for signature and does not have the force of law. Used to make policy changes that affect only the Congress.

of resolutions include legislation that organizes one chamber of Congress, that expresses the sense of one house or the other on a matter of public controversy, or that commends or censures a member of a chamber for his or her behavior. Resolutions receive the designation "H. Res." or "S. Res" as appropriate to the chamber where they are introduced.

Concurrent resolutions are similar to joint resolutions, in that they must be passed in identical form by both houses of Congress. However, unlike bills and joint resolutions, concurrent resolutions are not sent to the President for signature (in this sense, concurrent resolutions are similar to simple resolutions). Also, unlike bills and joint resolutions, concurrent resolutions—even when passed by both houses—do not have the force of law. Instead, these are used to express a sense of both houses of Congress, or to make a policy change that affects only the Congress, such as fixing a time for adjournment or creating joint committees within the Congress. Concurrent resolutions receive the designation "H.Con.Res." when they are introduced in the House and "S. Con. Res." when they are introduced in the Senate.

concurrent resolution Another type of legislation, similar to a joint resolution, that must be passed by both houses of Congress. However, it is not sent to the President for signature and does not have the force of law, even when passed in identical form. Concurrent resolutions are used to make policy changes that affect only the Congress.

Because the legislative process differs by type of legislation introduced, it is important to be familiar with the different types of proposals that members can introduce.

Members of Congress get ideas for legislation from a variety of places: their constituents, lobbyists, major events, and their own personal or professional experiences. Thus, as Congress, and the House in particular, more accurately

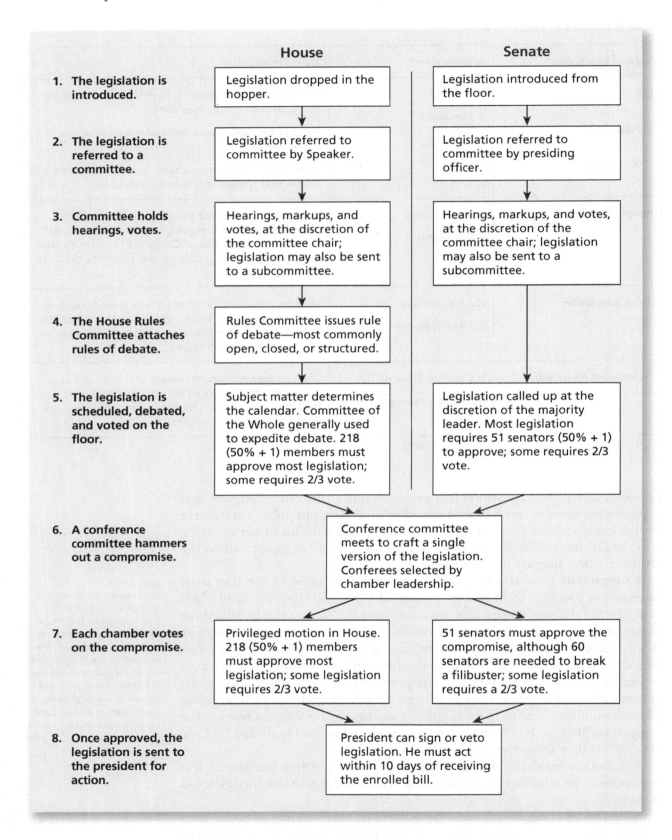

House

Senate

1. **The legislation is introduced.**

   Legislation dropped in the hopper.

   Legislation introduced from the floor.

2. **The legislation is referred to a committee.**

   Legislation referred to committee by Speaker.

   Legislation referred to committee by presiding officer.

3. **Committee holds hearings, votes.**

   Hearings, markups, and votes, at the discretion of the committee chair; legislation may also be sent to a subcommittee.

   Hearings, markups, and votes, at the discretion of the committee chair; legislation may also be sent to a subcommittee.

4. **The House Rules Committee attaches rules of debate.**

   Rules Committee issues rule of debate—most commonly open, closed, or structured.

5. **The legislation is scheduled, debated, and voted on the floor.**

   Subject matter determines the calendar. Committee of the Whole generally used to expedite debate. 218 (50% + 1) members must approve most legislation; some requires 2/3 vote.

   Legislation called up at the discretion of the majority leader. Most legislation requires 51 senators (50% + 1) to approve; some requires 2/3 vote.

6. **A conference committee hammers out a compromise.**

   Conference committee meets to craft a single version of the legislation. Conferees selected by chamber leadership.

7. **Each chamber votes on the compromise.**

   Privileged motion in House. 218 (50% + 1) members must approve most legislation; some legislation requires 2/3 vote.

   51 senators must approve the compromise, although 60 senators are needed to break a filibuster; some legislation requires a 2/3 vote.

8. **Once approved, the legislation is sent to the president for action.**

   President can sign or veto legislation. He must act within 10 days of receiving the enrolled bill.

Figure 2.1 The Textbook Legislative Process

reflects the diverse gender, race, and religious identities of the American people—what political scientists refer to as descriptive representation—the content of proposed legislation has become more diverse as well. Political scientists and Black/African American studies scholars Michael Minta and Nadia Brown summarize this point succinctly in their study of gender, race, and congressional issue attention, writing that: "descriptive representatives improve the substantive representation of their respective groups in the policy making process."[4] And political scientists Lisa Bryant and Julia Marin Hellwege find that members of Congress who are working mothers are more active at introducing legislation addressing issues relating to children and families than other legislators. In short, the more that Congress looks like America, the more likely it is that issues of importance to all Americans will find their way into the legislative process. At the same time, members remain under extraordinary pressure from lobbyists to introduce and support legislation that is of interest to the organizations they represent.[5]

2. The legislation is referred to a committee.

Regardless of subject matter, once a bill or resolution has been introduced, it is typically sent to a committee in the Congress to be processed. There are three main types of committees in Congress: **standing committees**, which are established to be permanent and with fixed jurisdictions; **select** or **special committees**, which are temporary committees set up to deal with a specific problem; and **joint committees**, which are committees—either standing or special—that include members of Congress from both chambers. In the House, legislation is almost always sent to at least one standing committee; the Speaker of the House ultimately determines the committee to which a bill or resolution will be referred. In the Senate, the presiding officer of the Senate makes the referral. In both chambers, however, the **parliamentarians** are integrally involved with decisions about bill referrals because a bill must be referred to the **committee of jurisdiction**—the standing committee that has jurisdiction over the subject matter of the legislation, as determined by the rules of the two chambers. In some cases, a piece of legislation can be referred to more than one committee. In the House, the Speaker of the House has discretion to refer the bill to more than one committee (a so-called **multiple referral**); in the Senate, multiple referrals are rare.[6]

At the start of the 117th Congress, the House had twenty standing committees and the Senate had sixteen standing committees. Figure 2.2 identifies each chamber's standing committees.

Each of the standing committees in the House and Senate sets its own rules (which can be reviewed by visiting the committees' websites at www.house.gov or www.senate.gov). Common to all committees, however, is that the chair of the committee has the greatest amount of control over the committee's agenda.

In addition to the standing committees of the House and Senate, there are a number of select and joint committees. Although these committees rarely consider legislative proposals, they may be used to provide guidance on policy initiatives or to gather information related to public policy making. At the beginning of the 117th Congress, they are:

descriptive representation The idea that members of Congress, whether individually or collectively, match the outward characteristics or typical experiences of the people they represent.

standing committee A committee of either the House of Representatives or the U.S. Senate whose jurisdiction is fixed according to the rules of the chamber. These committees are permanent in that they cannot be eliminated nor their jurisdiction changed without altering the standing rules of the chamber.

select (special) committee A committee, sometimes temporary, with limited jurisdiction. Select committees rarely consider legislative proposals but may provide policy guidance or conduct investigations.

joint committee A congressional committee made up of members of both the House and the Senate.

parliamentarian A nonpartisan expert on rules of parliamentary procedure and chamber precedent serving in either the House of Representatives or the Senate, whose job it is to advise the chamber leadership on process questions related to chamber rules and norms.

committee of jurisdiction The standing committee in the House or the Senate that has the responsibility, per the standing rules of the chamber, to hear a particular piece of legislation based upon its subject matter.

multiple referral The referral of a piece of legislation by the Speaker of the House or presiding officer of the Senate to more than one committee for processing.

House Permanent Select Committee on Intelligence

House Select Committee on the Climate Crisis

House Select Committee on Economic Disparity and Fairness in Growth

House Select Committee on the Modernization of Congress

Joint Select Committee on the Solvency of Multiemployer Pension Plans

Joint Committee on the Library

Joint Committee on Printing

Joint Committee on Taxation

Joint Economic Committee

Senate Select Committee on Ethics

Senate Select Committee on Intelligence

Senate Special Committee on Aging

Proposed legislation does not have to go to the same committee in the House that it goes to in the Senate. As should be clear from the information above, in some cases, there are not equivalent committees in each chamber.

Standing Committees in the 117th House	Standing Committees in the 117th Senate
Committee on Agriculture	Committee on Agriculture, Nutrition, and Forestry
Committee on Appropriations	Committee on Appropriations
Committee on Armed Services	Committee on Armed Services
Committee on the Budget	Committee on Banking, Housing, and Urban Affairs
Committee on Education and Labor	Committee on Budget
Committee on Energy and Commerce	Committee on Commerce, Science, and Transportation
Committee on Ethics	Committee on Energy and Natural Resources
Committee on Financial Services	Committee on Environment and Public Works
Committee on Foreign Affairs	Committee on Finance
Committee on Homeland Security	Committee on Foreign Relations
Committee on House Administration	Committee on Homeland Security and Governmental Affairs
Committee on the Judiciary	Committee on Health, Education, Labor, and Pensions
Committee on Natural Resources	Committee on Judiciary
Committee on Oversight and Reform	Committee on Rules and Administration
Committee on Rules	Committee on Small Business and Entrepreneurship
Committee on Science, Space, and Technology	Committee on Veterans' Affairs
Committee on Small Business	
Committee on Transportation and Infrastructure	
Committee on Veterans' Affairs	
Committee on Ways and Means	

Figure 2.2 Standing Committees in Congress, 117th Congress

Source: https://www.house.gov/committees and https://www.senate.gov/committees/index.htm.

Therefore, legislative proposals generally are sent to the committee that is most appropriate in the House and the committee that is most appropriate in the Senate, although there may also be strategic reasons for the committee referrals made by the chamber leadership.

3. The committee(s) of jurisdiction hold(s) hearings on the bill, debate(s) it, and then sometimes pass(es) it out of committee and back to the full House or Senate.

In the textbook model of the legislative process, the committee or committees of jurisdiction usually do the work of preparing a bill or resolution to be debated by the full chamber. As Professors Christopher Deering and Steven Smith write in *Committees in Congress*, "In the modern Congress, committees have three primary powers: collecting information through hearings and investigations, drafting the actual language of bills and resolutions, and reporting legislation to their parent chambers for consideration."[7] Every committee in the Congress is empowered to hold **hearings** on any proposals that are referred to it.

Committees also have the power to subpoena witnesses and documents that are deemed crucial to their work, although the nature and scope of Congress's subpoena power was narrowed by the Supreme Court in matters relating to the President in 2020. With the exception of the House and Senate Intelligence and Appropriations Committees, the hearings held by congressional committees are open to the public.

Once hearings are held, the committee may choose to hold a **markup** on the legislation. This is the time when members of the committee are able to amend the legislation to make it more acceptable to them. During the markup, the members of the committee meet to discuss their proposed amendments. This is a time to make changes to the existing language of the legislation. Depending on the subject matter and length of the legislation, the markup process can take a few hours or a few weeks.

Following the markup, the committee will schedule the bill or resolution for a vote. These votes take place during the committee's regularly scheduled executive business meeting. When it is time to vote, members of the committee who support the legislation will speak on its behalf and the members who oppose it will speak against it. Then the committee clerk will call the roll, and members will announce their decisions on the proposal. A majority of members of the committee must vote in favor of the legislation in order for it to be sent to the floor. Voting patterns in committee often reflect the partisan makeup of the committee itself, as the congressional parties have become more ideologically homogenous internally as well as more ideologically polarized from one another. Nevertheless, committee votes are not always along party lines. If there is a tie vote in committee, the bill or resolution is almost always dead. In rare cases, legislation will be sent to the full chamber even though it did not get a majority to support it in committee. These rare instances generally include such important legislative business as Supreme Court nominees in the Senate, or leadership priorities in both chambers. However, when a measure is advanced out of committee on a tie vote, it frequently indicates difficulty in the remaining steps in the legislative process.

hearing   A meeting at which members of Congress hear testimony and receive information and advice pertaining to proposed legislation or to an legislative inquiry or congressional investigation.

markup   in committee processing of legislation in which the members of the committee amend the pending legislation.

4. In the House, a bill passed by a standing committee is sent to the Rules Committee, where a rule of debate is attached.

Once legislation has been passed by the relevant committee(s) of jurisdiction in the House, it is sent to the House Rules Committee, whose job is to attach a rule of debate. The House Rules Committee serves to promote the interest of the majority party leadership, and for that reason, it is sometimes referred to as "the Speaker's Committee." The majority party dominates the Rules Committee with a supermajority of nine majority party members compared with only four minority party members. As a result, it is very difficult for the minority party to assert its will; to draft a rule for a bill that favors the minority party, the four minority party members would need to convince three majority party members of the committee to agree.

The Rules Committee can attach a number of rules; among the more common are open rules, modified open rules, structured rules, and closed rules.[8] **Open rules** permit any members to offer any germane amendments—those related to the subject matter of the measure—to the legislation when it is brought up for debate. **Modified open rules** permit some amendments, but may impose conditions on offering them and time limits that affect how many amendments ultimately may be considered. **Structured rules** are very specific about which amendments may be offered and under what time frame. **Closed rules** prohibit any amendments at all from being made to the legislation. In recent years, the House Rules Committee has essentially eliminated the use of open rules. Whereas in the 104th Congress (1995–96), 58 percent of all special rules were open or modified open; in the 115th and 116th Congresses, not a single open or modified rule was reported by the rules committee, and more than half of the rules reported in each Congress (56 percent and 54 percent, respectively) were closed rules.[9]

Once the Rules Committee has approved a rule of debate, the rule must be approved by a majority of the full House in order for the legislation to be considered. If the rule fails in the House, the legislation to which it was attached is considered to be dead as well. This is because there is no mechanism to determine how debate on the measure will proceed in the absence of a rule. However, as Oleszek explains, the House rarely fails to approve a rule; it is an expectation that majority party members will support the rules worked out by the House Rules Committee.[10]

5. The bill is scheduled on the House or Senate floor, where it is then debated and voted on before being sent to the other chamber for approval.

Once a rule has been attached to a piece of pending legislation, that legislation is eligible to be scheduled for floor debate. Although scheduling legislation seems as though it ought to be a simple process, in reality scheduling legislation can be quite complicated. For example, the House has five different calendars. The **union calendar** is reserved for bills that deal with revenues and expenditures, including taxation and appropriations bills. The **house calendar** is reserved for nonmoney bills of major importance; most substantive measures will be placed on this calendar. The **corrections calendar** is used for noncontroversial measures that address

---

open rule A rule of debate in the House of Representatives that permits any member of the House to offer any germane amendment to the pending legislation.

modified open rule A rule of debate in the House of Representatives that permits some amendments to pending legislation, but usually imposes requirements and time limits on the offering of amendments.

structured rule A rule of debate in the House of Representatives that specifies very clearly what amendments may be offered to legislation and provides strict time frames for consideration.

closed rule A rule of debate in the House of Representatives that prohibits nearly all amendments from being made to the pending legislation.

union calendar A calendar used by the House of Representatives that is reserved for bills that deal with revenues and expenditures, including taxation and appropriations bills.

house calendar A calendar used by the House of Representatives that is reserved for nonmoney bills of major importance. Most substantive measures are placed on this calendar.

corrections calendar A calendar used by the House of Representatives for noncontroversial measures. Measures on this calendar can only be brought up on certain days of the month, at the Speaker's discretion.

"laws and regulations that are ambiguous, arbitrary, or ludicrous."[11] Measures on this calendar can only be brought up on certain days of the month—generally, the second and fourth Tuesdays, at the discretion of the Speaker of the House.[12] The **private calendar** is used to schedule private bills, which were previously discussed. Like the corrections calendar, this calendar is only in order on certain days of the month—generally the first and third Tuesdays of the month, although this is also at the Speaker's discretion.[13] Finally, the **discharge calendar** is used to schedule legislation that has been forced out of committee through a **discharge petition**.[14]

Once legislation has been placed on one of these House calendars, it can be called up for consideration at the discretion of the Speaker of the House. The Speaker is not obligated to call up the legislation in the order in which it was placed on the calendar; in fact, policy and political considerations are far more likely to determine the order by which the House considers legislation.

The House adds another complication to the debate and passage of legislation: the Committee of the Whole House on the State of the Union. The **Committee of the Whole**, as it is called, is a procedural device designed to enhance the legislative process in the House. The Committee of the Whole, like the House of Representatives itself, meets in the House chamber, but it uses procedures designed to expedite the amendment process. Indeed, most legislation is actually debated in the Committee of the Whole, which requires a quorum of 100 (as compared with the House of Representatives, which requires a quorum of 218). There are also very strict time constraints imposed in the Committee of the Whole, limiting the amount of time for the offering of amendments. Meeting as the Committee of the Whole permits the House to make significantly more progress on pending legislation than it could possibly make if it used the rules of the House to structure debate, because the debate rules used by the full House can be manipulated much more easily to prevent the passage of legislation.

Once the work of amending the legislation is done, the Committee of the Whole reports the amended measure back to the House of Representatives, which must then vote to accept the amendments. This process is sometimes confusing to outsiders because the very same members who voted to approve the amendments in the Committee of the Whole vote again to approve them in the House of Representatives. One surefire way to tell whether the members are meeting in the Committee of the Whole or in the House of Representatives is to look at the mace, a tall staff that sits near the Speaker's right hand that symbolizes the authority of the House of Representatives. When the mace is in the upper position, the members are meeting as the House of Representatives. When the mace is lowered, the members are meeting in the Committee of the Whole.

In contrast to the complex and formal legislative procedure of the House, the Senate uses less-complicated and less-structured rules of procedure. Instead of the varied calendars of the House, the Senate has only two calendars. Nearly all the legislative business of the Senate is scheduled on the **legislative calendar**, with the exception of treaties and presidential nominations, which are placed on the **executive calendar**. Unlike the House, the Senate switches easily between calendars at the discretion of the **majority leader**. In the Senate, legislation is

private calendar A calendar used by the House of Representatives to schedule private bills. Like the corrections calendar, the private calendar is only in order on certain days of the month, at the Speaker's discretion.

discharge calendar A calendar used by the House of Representatives to schedule legislation that has been forced out of committee through a discharge petition.

discharge petition A petition of 218 members of the House of Representatives that forces a piece of legislation out of committee over the objection of the committee's members or the committee chair. This is often used to circumvent committee chairs' prerogative to determine whether or not to move a piece of legislation to a committee vote.

Committee of the Whole Short for Committee of the Whole House on the State of the Union, the Committee of the Whole is used for floor debate in the House of Representatives. There are significant procedural advantages to meeting as the Committee of the Whole, including expedited rules of debate and relaxed requirements for a quorum.

legislative calendar One of two calendars used by the U.S. Senate. This calendar is used for scheduling legislative proposals.

executive calendar The second of two calendars used by the U.S. Senate. This calendar is used for scheduling executive branch items that require the Senate's approval, such as nominations to the executive and judicial branches, and treaties.

majority leader Floor leader of the majority party in both the House and the Senate. This individual is responsible for managing floor debate for the majority party.

minority leader   Floor leader of the minority party in both the House and the Senate. This individual manages floor debate for the minority party.

unanimous consent request   In the context of scheduling legislation, a request from the majority leader to the rest of the senators in the chamber to consider a piece of legislation. In other contexts, a unanimous consent request is a request made by any member of the Senate to his or her fellow senators asking that all senators agree to whatever the senator has proposed to do.

motion to proceed   A parliamentary motion used to call up a measure for consideration.

unanimous consent agreement   An agreement negotiated between the Senate majority and minority leaders agreeing to bring up an item of pending business and agreeing to specific terms of debate. These agreements, at least theoretically, indicate that no member of the Senate from either party will object to the terms of debate agreed to by the leadership.

hold   A request from a senator to the majority leader not to bring a piece of pending legislation to the floor for a vote.

filibuster   A procedural delaying tactic in the U.S. Senate that allows a single senator, or a small group of senators, to block action on pending business with which they disagree by speaking continuously and refusing the yield the floor. A supermajority vote of 60 senators is required in order to end a filibuster.

amendment tree   A visual representation of the order of voting on proposed amendments to an item of pending legislative business.

brought to the floor either through a **unanimous consent request**, which is a request to the chamber from the majority leader to consider a piece of legislation and is typically used for noncontroversial measures or on a **motion to proceed** to consideration. Since the objection of a single senator can prevent legislation from being brought up, unanimous consent requests are used only when the majority leader is certain that the entire membership of the Senate is willing to proceed to consideration of a bill or resolution. As there is no Rules Committee in the Senate, the terms of debate may be set through a **unanimous consent agreement**, which is an agreement between the **majority leader** and the **minority leader** setting the terms of debate and time limits for consideration of the measure.

Unanimous consent agreements are made between the majority leader, the minority leader, committee chairs, and any senators with an interest in the pending legislation.[15] The purpose of these agreements is to avoid obstruction and delay from obstinate senators. These obstructionist tactics can take the form of **holds**—requests to the majority leader not to bring legislation or nominations to the floor for a vote—or **filibusters**. Unanimous consent agreements also specify the time and date that debate on a measure will begin.

Once legislation has been scheduled in the chamber, it will be brought to the floor under the procedures specified by the Rules Committee (in the House) or by the unanimous consent agreement (in the Senate). During floor debate in the House, only germane amendments—those related to the subject matter of the legislation—are permitted and are debated subject to the rule attached by the Rules Committee. The Senate does not have a germaneness requirement, which means that any amendment that a senator wishes to offer will be in order. In both the House and the Senate, the amending process is governed by the **amendment tree**, so called because when drawn, it looks like a tree trunk with many protruding branches. The amendment tree specifies the nature of amendments and the order in which they will be voted upon.

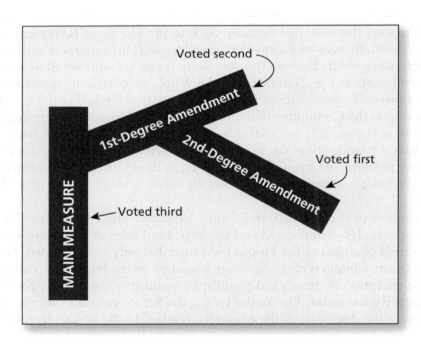

Figure 2.3 Amendment Tree

Although the amendment tree shown in Figure 2.3 is oversimplified, it illustrates the major principles of voting on amendments to legislation. Second-degree amendments are the first amendments to be voted on, because they affect the content of the first-degree amendments. Once the second-degree amendments have been disposed of, the first-degree amendments are acted on. It is also important to note that there are two kinds of first-degree amendments: perfecting and substitute amendments. **Substitute amendments** strike one or more sections of a piece of legislation and replace them wholesale with new language. **Perfecting amendments** seek to adapt the existing language of a section or sections to be more acceptable to members of the House or the Senate.

In both the House and the Senate, most legislation requires only a majority vote to be approved. There are a few exceptions to this rule, however. For example, rules change and new taxation proposals require a supermajority vote in the Senate. Once the bill or resolution is passed by one chamber, the other chamber must pass it in identical form.

6. If the two chambers pass different versions, they must reconcile the differences.

It is unusual for a measure to pass both chambers in identical form because the House and Senate use different procedures and have different rules. But the Presentment Clause of the U.S. Constitution (Article I, Section 7) requires that Congress submit a single version of a measure to the President. Traditionally, the mechanism used by Congress to reconcile chamber differences was a conference committee. **Conference committees** are temporary committees consisting of members of both the House and the Senate. Conference committees allow members of both chambers to meet together to reach a consensus version of the measure. When conference committees are used, the Speaker of the House formally selects House conferees; Senate conferees are formally selected by the majority leader. In both chambers, the conferees generally come from the standing committee that had jurisdiction over the legislation and that originally considered the proposal. Conference committees usually consist of anywhere from five to twenty members, although there have been conference committees with well over 100 members sitting as conferees. For example, Sinclair notes that the conference committee for a 1988 trade bill had 199 conferees.[16]

Conference committees wield a tremendous amount of power. They have the ability to dramatically alter legislation and their work product—the final conference report that refers the legislation back to each chamber for a final vote—is sent back to both chambers as a **privileged motion**, meaning the legislation can no longer be amended. Once this privileged bill is back on the House or Senate floor, it is rare that either chamber will vote to reject it, because by that time it is a completed piece of legislation. Neither chamber can amend the legislation nor can either chamber vote to reject it; if either of those events happens, the legislation is dead.

Conference committees are no longer used very frequently. Conference committees are slow and in the Senate it is possible to filibuster the motion to send legislation to conference, making the process of even to getting to conference difficult. In addition, the scarcity of legislative time and the leadership's desire to control legislative outcomes make it much more common—and more expeditious—for Congress to use other methods of reconciling

substitute amendment An amendment that strikes a section or sections of pending legislation and replaces what was stricken with entirely new language.

perfecting amendment An amendment that adapts, but does not take the place of, the existing language of the proposed measure.

conference committee A temporary, joint committee made up of members of both the House and the Senate. The purpose of these committees is to resolve differences in legislation passed by both the House and the Senate. The conference committee is typically the last step before final passage of a piece of legislation in the U.S. Congress.

privileged motion A motion that must be addressed ahead of all other pending motions.

ping-ponging   The process of reconciling House and Senate legislative differences by sending successive drafts of measures back and forth to each chamber for approval until a single consensus draft emerges.

enrolled bill   Legislation passed in identical form by both the House of Representatives and the U.S. Senate.

pocket veto   Once both houses of Congress pass a piece of legislation in identical form, the President has ten days to sign it into law or veto it. If Congress adjourns during that ten-day period and the President has not acted, the measure does not become law.

differences. The two most common mechanisms are for one chamber to simply pass the other chamber's version of the legislation or for the two chambers to engage in "ping-ponging" whereby successive versions of the legislation are passed back and forth between the chambers until a single consensus version emerges.[17] In both cases, informal negotiation between the chambers' leaders may also take place to facilitate the process of achieving agreement.

7. Once the bill passes each chamber in identical form, it is sent to the President for approval.

Once a bill or resolution passes both chambers in identical form, the **enrolled bill** is sent to the President, who has ten days to decide whether to sign it into law, veto it, or do nothing. If the President signs it, the text becomes law according to the provisions of the legislation. To veto the legislation, the President pens a veto message and returns the legislation to the Secretary of the House and Secretary of the Senate. If the President does nothing, the legislation either dies or becomes law without signature, depending on whether Congress adjourns during the ten days set aside for the President to act. If the Congress remains in session and the President fails to act, the proposal will become law without signature. If Congress adjourns before the President has acted, the measure is dead. This latter circumstance is known as a **pocket veto**.

Unorthodox Lawmaking

After this section, you will be able to:

- Identify the ways in which "textbook" Congress has yielded to "unorthodox lawmaking" in the legislative process.

- Describe the ways in which changes to the legislative process have had implications for the types of laws that are passed by Congress.

Although the information provided by the textbook model of the legislative process is informative, it neglects many of the political realities of the contemporary Congress. One of the most important changes to the legislative process is the extent to which the chamber leadership has replaced committees as the driving forces behind legislating in Congress. Today, chamber leaders exercise far more control over the substance and timing of legislation than they have in at least a century. The coalescence of power in the chamber leadership is partly a reflection of the ways in which rank-and-file members' time commitments have changed; today, members are expected to spend a significant amount of their time fundraising, which has pushed legislating to the back burner for many members. But, as political scientists Gary Cox and Mathew McCubbins have argued, the centrality of the leadership is also the result of the political parties in Congress now operating as "legislative cartels," in which the leaders of congressional parties seek to control and enhance the party brand by pursuing policies that enhance their members' electoral prospects.[18] The now-central role of party leaders in setting the legislative agenda has ripple effects for members' own decisions about what policies to pursue and how to allocate their time and efforts. Finally, the textbook version of the process also neglects the political environment that constrains legislators and influences their behavior. All of these changing circumstances make it necessary to consider the ways in which the textbook model is no longer sufficient for understanding how Congress works.

Shifting Agenda Control

Over the last four decades there has been a fundamental shift from committee-centered legislating to leadership-centered policy making. Sinclair identified this trend toward leadership-centered control over legislation in the late 1990s, but by then it had already been in the works for nearly twenty years. For example, looking at the period between 1981 and 2005, congressional scholar Frances Lee found that appropriations of funds to support leadership offices grew at twice the rate of legislative branch appropriations more generally.[19]

Although the textbook version of the legislative process emphasizes committees as wielding enormous influence over what legislation Congress takes up, increasingly committees are being bypassed as chamber leaders seek greater control over the legislative agenda. Sinclair notes that between 2007 and 2014, as many as one in three measures bypassed the congressional committee stage and went straight to the House floor for a vote.[20]

When measures bypass the committee stage, it is because the chamber leadership wants to exercise control over the content and timing of the legislation. As political scientist James Curry notes in *Legislating in the Dark,* congressional leaders engage in activities including "drafting bills behind closed doors and keeping legislative language secret throughout most of the process, changing the contents of legislation immediately before consideration in committee or on the floor, and exploiting or exacerbating the complexity of the legislation and legislative language"[21] in order to ensure that rank-and-file members are reliant on them for information and cues about how to vote. **Legislative cue taking** is not new; with thousands of pieces of legislation to vote on annually, members cannot possibly know enough about each one to make an independent judgment about how to vote. But the great extent to which chamber leaders now exercise control over the legislative agenda and bypass the public phases of legislative review that historically took place in committees represents a fundamental change from the textbook legislative process that was discussed earlier in this chapter.

The shift away from using committees to consider and craft important legislation means that committee work is increasingly devoted to oversight and investigations rather than processing legislation. Many members of Congress now use committee hearings as opportunities to score political points or make a name for themselves. Congressional committees now hold fewer hearings and call far fewer witnesses than at any point in the last four decades, reducing information flow into the legislative process and reducing the public's ability to learn about measures under consideration.[22] Beyond dampening the public's engagement in policy making, leadership-centered lawmaking disincentivizes even Congress's own members from investing time and energy into legislation. For example, in January 2021, Madison Cauthorn (R-NC), a new member of Congress, wrote in an e-mail to his Republican colleagues: "I have built my staff around comms rather than legislation."[23] This is possible because in the

legislative cue taking The practice of members of Congress seeking advice from like-minded interest groups and fellow members about how to vote on a piece of legislation.

contemporary Congress, significant legislative work is done by the leadership, further reducing individual member incentives to engage in lawmaking.

In the House of Representatives, the centrality of the leadership in the lawmaking process also has implications for the Rules Committee's work. Not only do leaders seek to control the language of the measures being debated but they also seek to ensure that their preferred version of legislation survives debate on the floor by limiting the amount of time measures are debated and which amendments, if any, may be offered. Over the last three decades, the House Rules Committee has increased its use of mechanisms such as **self-executing rules** and other restrictive debate-structuring devices in order to give chamber leaders significant leverage over the final format of legislation they care about.[24]

Changing Legislation

The leadership's much more substantial involvement in the legislative process has had important implications for the nature and type of legislation introduced by members and considered in committees. While the process of introducing legislation is the same—bills today are still dropped in the hopper in the House and announced from the floor in the Senate—the substance and form of the legislation that gets introduced has changed in important ways that affect the ways Congress carries out the remainder of its work in the legislative process. As GovTrack.us notes, Congress is enacting roughly the same quantity of law that it always has, but it now does it in fewer but longer pieces of legislation[25] that can reach several thousands of pages for major legislation.[26] Some of these longer measures are examples of **omnibus legislation**—"legislation that addresses numerous and not necessarily related subjects, issues, and programs, and therefore is usually highly complex and long."[27] Political scientist Glen Krutz notes that members of Congress have increased their use of omnibus legislation because it has proven to be an efficient way of getting around partisan gridlock. Controversial provisions are frequently accepted without question because of the need to pass the major provisions of the omnibus bills. Omnibus legislation is appealing to members because it can provide them with political cover; rather than explaining their vote on a controversial provision, they can focus on the noncontroversial or more significant aspects of the legislation to divert attention from the parts of the legislation about which their constituents would be unhappy.[28]

In addition to lengthier and more complicated legislation, some aspects of the content of legislation have also changed. From 2011 until 2020, **earmarks**—specific appropriations targeted at a member's district—were banned, mostly eliminating this targeted spending from pending legislation. While proponents of the earmarks ban celebrated the removal of what they considered to be wasteful spending from legislation, many congressional scholars noted that earmarks were often an effective vehicle for funding projects that were important to members' constituents.[29] Many members themselves felt this way about earmarks, too, but felt forced to vote to eliminate them in 2011 out of fears that they would be labeled as wasteful spenders if they did not.

Eliminating earmarks changed the calculus for members about what votes they would be able to explain to their constituents and reduced the ability of members to engage in **logrolling**—supporting one another's legislative proposals in exchange for a benefit or support on one's own priorities—to help pass legislation. And, the elimination of earmarks reduced members'

self-executing rule A special rule used by the House Rules Committee stating that when the rule is adopted, the House is "deemed" to have taken another action on which the House did not vote directly.

omnibus legislation Complicated and lengthy legislative proposals that address substantial numbers of public policy questions in a single measure.

earmark Targeted appropriation by Congress directing funds to be spent on a specific project, often aimed at securing a member's or members' votes by directing funds to projects of importance to their constituents.

logrolling The practice of legislators trading favors and votes in order to secure support for their proposals and priorities.

engagement with pending legislation, as they had fewer incentives to monitor legislation closely to ensure their concerns were being addressed. At the start of the 117th Congress, Democrats in the House announced that they would permit earmarking to begin again, but within limits and with improved transparency.[30]

Finally, as noted earlier, the changing composition of Congress, with greater numbers of women and persons of color, especially in the House of Representatives, has had important consequences for the content of legislation introduced and the ways in which members prioritize engagement in legislating. As political scientists Carly Schmitt and Hanna Brant write: "In short, women legislators are critical in advocating and promoting policies that directly impact women and children, and as history has shown, without women in elected office these issues would be largely ignored."[31]

Similarly, political scientist Sara Angevine finds that female-identifying members' representation of women's interests extends to the interests of global women, much as previous research has shown that African American members of Congress have acted as "transnational surrogates" for Africa-related foreign policy considerations.[32]

High Levels of Partisanship and Obstruction

Partisanship in Congress has increased in the Congress in recent years. Although partisanship has always been important in the House because that chamber's rules are organized to promote the interests of the majority party, as previously noted, partisanship and party polarization have reached all-time highs in both the House and the Senate. Today, congressional scholars don't just talk about partisanship as characterizing Congress, they also focus on the polarization that has occurred between the two major parties, both outside and within the Congress.

Polarization is problematic because it means that not only do the two parties in Congress collectively have different viewpoints, it means that there are no longer very many members of either party who are moderate enough to build bridges between the parties in order to make public policy. Consider, for example, that the Voting Rights Act of 1965 passed with overwhelming bipartisan support, with 78 percent of Democrats and 83 percent of Republicans voting in favor of passing this sweeping voting rights legislation at a time when civil rights for all Americans were far from universally accepted.[33] By comparison, in March 2021, 99.5 percent of Democrats but zero Republicans voted in favor of the For the People Act aimed at promoting election integrity, ensuring the right to vote for all citizens, and promoting ethics in government.[34]

Party polarization has consequences for the ability of Congress to act and for the durability of the laws it is able to pass. For example, when the chambers are nearly evenly split, as was the case for the 117th Congress, with 50 Republican and 50 Democratic senators, and the House Democratic majority controlling just 50.8 percent of seats in the chamber, reaching a majority to approve new laws is extremely difficult. When laws are passed with votes exclusively from one party, achieving public support for their implementation or ensuring that the policy is lasting and stable may be impossible. The 2010 Patient Protection and Affordable Care Act is an example of this. Passed with zero Republican votes in either the U.S. House or U.S. Senate during the 111th Congress, House Republicans tried more than 70 times to repeal the law during the next eight years when they were in control of the chamber.[35] As political scientists Logan Dancey and Geoffrey

Sheagley explain: "Although debate exists over the causes and consequences of congressional polarization, a scholarly consensus has emerged that the contemporary Congress is among the most polarized in history."[36]

Along with polarization, obstructive behavior in the U.S. Senate has reached new heights in recent years as well. As noted previously in this chapter, holds and filibusters have long been possible in the chamber. But, for most of the Senate's history, these tactics were used sparingly. Senate norms of respect for colleagues and deference to more senior senators—especially to the chamber's leaders—meant that senators were generally reluctant to obstruct. In the contemporary Senate, the threat of obstruction is omnipresent, with senators being increasingly willing to try to bring the chamber's business to a halt if they believe it will advance their political interests. An increase in obstructive behavior began in earnest in the early 1970s; in response, time-consuming but strategic efforts to prevent obstruction by the leadership ramped up in the 1990s. The threat of a filibuster even over business that was once routine, such as appointing conferees to conference committees, is one reason that conference committees are no longer widely used to reconcile differences between House and Senate versions of legislation. At the start of the 117th Congress, a number of prominent Democrats both in the Senate and outside it called for reform or even the abolition of the filibuster in order to allow President Joe Biden's legislative priorities to move forward in the Senate, but even if such reforms were to be successful, there are other methods of obstruction available to determined senators.

Figure 2.4 shows one way that increasing obstruction has manifested in the modern Senate. Fifty years ago, **cloture motions** aimed at ending extended debate were brought to the floor by any senator who wished to move on from the obstruction. Over time, the cloture motion has become a tool used exclusively by the Senate Majority Leader to control floor time and ensure that obstructionists cannot hijack Senate proceedings. These days, when the majority leader calls up legislation for debate on the floor, a cloture motion limiting the amount of time for debate will almost always be filed at the same time. Senate leaders say this is necessary to prevent obstructionists from thwarting the chamber's work, but critics say that the consequence is the lack of real, substantive debate on legislation pending in the chamber.

cloture motion A motion brought before the Senate to end a filibuster or prevent extended debate. Sixteen senators must request the motion, and a supermajority—sixty senators—must agree.

The Political Environment

There have not only been significant changes to the legislative process within Congress, but there have been concomitant changes to the political and media environment within which Congress operates that have, in turn, affected the way Congress conducts its work.

One significant change is the extent to which members of Congress are engaged in a permanent campaign for reelection. In 2013, *Washington Post* staff writer Ezra Klein reported that the Democratic Congressional Campaign Committee (DCCC) was encouraging Democratic members to spend four hours a day on "call time"—a catchphrase that means fundraising.[37] In the 2018 congressional midterms, the average Senate winner spent nearly $16 million while the average House winner spent nearly $2 million.[38] At that rate House members need to raise approximately $2,800 *per day, every day* during their two-year term. This is why members spend so much time on fundraising activities. This pressing

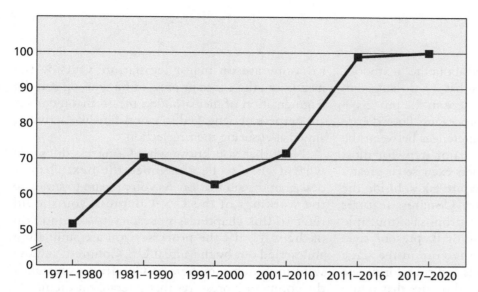

Figure 2.4 Proportion of Cloture Motions Filed by Senate Majority Leader, 1971–2021

Source: Compiled by author from U.S. Senate cloture data available online (see individual congress data at http://www.senate.gov/pagelayout/reference/cloture_motions/clotureCounts.htm).

need to raise funds reinforces the benefits to rank-and-file members of having chamber leaders take on more of the work of legislating.

Another important change to the political environment is in the way that members are able to share information about their work on the Hill with their constituents at home. The media landscape for members of Congress is now quite different from what it used to be. While historically members of Congress had limited opportunities to gain attention in the media, social media has transformed members' abilities to reach their constituents and to build a national following.[39] For example, New York's 14th congressional district representative Alexandria Ocasio-Cortez had more than 12.5 million followers on Twitter at the start of just her third year in office. For reference, the total population of the 14th congressional district was just under 721,000 in 2019.[40] This example illustrates the changing incentive structures that now operate on members of Congress. With party leaders controlling most significant legislation, and members expected to fundraise continuously, members are incentivized and rewarded for quickly and regularly gaining attention especially for appearing to speak truth to power, rather than for their legislative efforts or expertise—as the previous examples of Madison Cauthorne (R-NC) and Alexandria Ocasio Cortez (D-NY) demonstrate.

Chapter Summary

In this chapter, you have learned about the "textbook" legislative process and the ways that it has changed in recent years. While the major steps in the process—bill introduction, committee processing, floor debate and voting, and reconciling differences between the two chambers—are still the major steps for most legislation, today chamber leaders exercise far greater control over the course a measure takes. Inside the institution, the contemporary Congress features fewer, but longer, legislative proposals, multiple pathways through the House of Representatives that may include bypassing the committee stage altogether, restrictive time limits and rules for debate in both chambers, and polarized parties that refuse to cooperate on major legislation. Outside the institution, the constant press of fundraising and the fragmentation of media outlets means that members are perpetually engaged in campaign-like activities aimed at ensuring their reelection.

Now that you know what Congress does and what it's like to be a member, the next chapter describes the simulation. As you prepare to simulate the workings of the U.S. Congress, you should refer to this chapter as necessary to remind you of the ways that the processes you are simulating are carried out by the actual U.S. Congress, and the ways in which members of Congress experience the competing pressures that operate on them.

Key Terms

bill   10
public bill   10
private bill   10
joint resolution   10
simple resolution   10
concurrent resolution   11
descriptive representation   13
standing committee   13
select (special) committee   13
joint committee   13
parliamentarian   13
committee of jurisdiction   13
multiple referral   13
hearing   15
open rule   16
modified open rule   16
structured rule   16
closed rule   16
union calendar   16
house calendar   16
corrections calendar   16
private calendar   17
discharge calendar   17
discharge petition   17

Committee of the Whole   17
legislative calendar   17
executive calendar   17
majority leader   17
minority leader   18
unanimous consent request   18
motion to proceed   18
unanimous consent agreement   18
hold   18
filibuster   18
amendment tree   18
substitute amendment   19
perfecting amendment   19
conference committee   19
privileged motion   19
ping-ponging   20
enrolled bill   20
pocket veto   20
legislative cue taking   21
self-executing rule   22
omnibus legislation   22
earmark   22
logrolling   22
cloture motion   24

3

The Simulation

Learning Objectives

After this chapter, you will be able to:

- Explain how members of Congress's different backgrounds affect their approach to lawmaking and representation.

- Recognize the major components of legislation.

- Identify and explain the role of parties/partisanship, chamber leaders, and congressional committees in shaping legislative outputs in the U.S. House of Representatives.

- Discuss the ways in which legislative procedure influences legislative outcomes.

- Role-play a member of Congress and use the information you have learned about him or her to inform your choices and actions.

- Assess the difficult choices that members of Congress have to make.

- Articulate and evaluate the factors that affect members' actions and choices.

ongratulations on your election to the U.S. Congress! Now that you've been elected, you have new challenges to face. Not only do you have to meet the daily demands of reviewing legislation, supervising your staff, meeting with lobbyists, responding to media inquiries, fundraising, and working with other members of Congress, you are now accountable to your constituents as well. Constituents generally demand that their representatives do something for them, and members of Congress will, if they want to be reelected. "Doing something" includes such legislative activities as procuring resources, goods, or services for the district, providing essential services, and assisting constituents with understanding federal programs. The activities in this simulation also assume that each of you, at some point in the simulation, will fit David Mayhew's description of members of Congress as "single-minded seekers of reelection"[1] because unless you are reelected, you will not be able to pursue your other policy goals. The bottom line is that now it's time to get to work.

As a member of Congress in this simulation you will draft a legislative proposal, a justification for that proposal, and a Dear Colleague letter to seek support from other members of Congress. In addition, you will be expected to contribute to any and all party caucus and/or committee meetings, and to be present and play a part in floor debate and the debate over final passage of all legislation. In addition, participants may be called on to testify as a witness during the hearings held by their congressional committees, or by any other committees, throughout the semester. Remember that passage of your bill by the committee of jurisdiction and by the full House may depend wholly on your ability to persuade your colleagues. Finally, you'll be called on to explain yourselves to your constituents. As the late Richard Fenno explained in *Home Style: House Members in Their Districts*, members of Congress spend much of their time back in their districts explaining their work in Washington and their legislative voting decisions to their constituents. Your instructor will determine the precise nature of this assignment, but members engage in this work in a variety of ways, including through direct mail, media spots, and town hall-style meetings.

This simulation is intended to be an enjoyable and thought-provoking way to learn about the legislative process. Your instructor will act as the Speaker of the House, and it will also be your instructor's role to monitor your progress and help you acquire the resources you need to perform your duties as a member of Congress. In that sense, your instructor will from time to time fulfill roles that, in the real Congress, would be carried out by staff. (Of course, some of the tasks you'll be doing—such as actually drafting legislation—are also done primarily by staff in the real Congress.)

Your instructor will also set the specific policies and procedures related to the evaluation, grading, and weighting of the simulation assignments. In some cases, your instructor may opt to change or omit procedures that are specified in this chapter in order to make the simulation run smoothly. For that reason, you'll need to pay particular attention to the Speaker—just as the members of the actual U.S. House of Representatives must pay attention to the Speaker if they want to be certain to accomplish their goals.

To get started, you first need to decide who you are! To get you thinking about what sort of member of Congress you want to be, the next section describes the membership of the current Congress. At the end of the section, it will be time for you to make some decisions about whom you would like to portray.

Who Are the Members of Congress?

As noted in Chapter 1 members of Congress (also known as MCs) come from varied and diverse backgrounds. There is no one path to the U.S. Congress, although there are several common ways that members get to Capitol Hill—frequently through careers in business or the law.

Congressional scholars have explored the question "Who runs for Congress?" and have delved into the motivations of congressional candidates to understand what motivates some people to run for the U.S. House or Senate. Most congressional scholars agree that the people who choose to run are ambitious, believe that they can win the election, and are good fundraisers. Many begin their careers in local or state politics where they hone the needed campaigning and fundraising skills to contest a congressional election.[2] Congressional candidates also consider the national climate in making their decisions to run. As two congressional scholars note:

Politicians do act strategically. Their career decisions are influenced by their assessment of a variable political environment. Their choices reflect, among other things, the conventional wisdom that national events and conditions affect individual voting behavior. National phenomena thought to be important are consistently monitored and noted; indicators abound. More and better candidates appear when signs are favorable, worse and fewer when they are unfavorable.[3]

In the conclusion to his edited volume *Who Runs for Congress*, Thomas Kazee notes that those who run for Congress—who, ultimately, become members of Congress—are ambitious entrepreneurs who run because they believe they can win, and who often put personal and career interests on hold in order to seek elective office.[4] They frequently want to stay in the Congress for a reasonably lengthy period of time and will mold their constituency styles and congressional career in order to continue to be elected.[5] In short, many of today's members of Congress are highly political people. At the very least, many of them are "second-career" politicians, a term I use to mean those members of Congress who, having worked for a while in a particular career, leave that career to devote their remaining working years to public service as a member of Congress.

Kazee's text, published more than a quarter century ago, also concluded that in general those individuals who decide to run for a seat in Congress are "serious politicians," for whom "politics is at the center of their lives."[6] But this assessment no longer holds as true as it once did. Recent accounts in the popular press suggest that some number of candidates run for congressional office hoping to be elected to *prevent* government from acting (one recent editorial went as far as to call this group "a bonkers squad of media-thirsty political exhibitionists"[7]). And a recent study by political scientists Eric Hansen and Sarah Treul found that voters no longer value political experience when considering for whom to vote in congressional elections.[8]

Today's congressional membership remains dominated by male-identifying people who come from careers in fields like law and business, although Congress is less dominated by this archetypal member than it was a quarter century ago. Although the Congress is a long way from representing descriptively the diverse age, race, gender, economic, and labor background of the U.S. population as a whole, it is more descriptively representative now than it was a decade ago. The 2021 Congressional Research Service (CRS) report "Membership of the 117th Congress: A Profile" notes that at the start of the most recent Congress there were:

~145 female-identifying members (121 in the House, 24 in the Senate).

~54 Hispanic or Latino members (47 in the House, 7 in the Senate).

~60 African American members (57 in the House, 3 in the Senate.

~20 Asian/Pacific Islanders (18 in the House, 2 in the Senate).

~5 Native Americans in the House of Representatives.[9]

Many of these numbers represent significant gains in descriptive representation; and two—the number of Hispanic/Latino members and the number of Native American members—represent all-time records for the number of members from this demographic group. The number of women in Congress has doubled from what it was two decades ago, such that women now make up approximately 25 percent of those serving in Congress. This is a far cry from proportional representation (women have been between 50 and 51 percent of the population since at least the 1960s[10]) but it is significantly higher than the roughly 13 percent of seats held by women in the late 1990s.

While Congress looks more like America than it did twenty years ago, the average length of service for members of both chambers has stayed roughly flat over the same time period. The average length of prior service for members of the 117th House was nine years, and the average tenure for senators at the start of the 117th Senate was approximately eleven years.[11] The average age of members across both houses has been increasing over the last twenty years; at the start of the 117th Congress, the average age of members across both chambers was close to 60 years old. Representative Madison Cawthorn was the youngest member of Congress at 25—just meeting the constitutionally-prescribed minimum age—and Representative Don Young (R–AK) was the oldest at 87.[12]

The 117th Congress includes 13 former state governors and 10 former lieutenant governors as well as 238 former state legislators, 78 former congressional staff members, 38 former mayors, and several other members with previous experience in a state or local governing capacity.[13] A significant number of members also come from the business, education, health care, and legal professions. Approximately 17 percent of all members of Congress have served in the military, the lowest proportion of members with military experience since before World War II (e.g., in 1981–82, 64 percent of all members had prior military service).[14] In addition, the CRS Report finds that several members of Congress come from interesting and diverse backgrounds, noting that the occupations of the members of the 117th Congress include:

> an astronaut, a brew pub owner, professional football player, two broadcasters, a rodeo announcer, a television reporter, a video game developer, a carpenter, an animal nutrition specialist, a waiter, two documentary filmmakers, two radio talk show hosts, an FBI agent, a mixed martial arts fighter, a software engineer, and an explosives expert.[15]

The diverse backgrounds of members should not be surprising in light of the incredibly diverse backgrounds of the American people.

Simulation Assignment 1: Selecting a Member of Congress

In this assignment you will:

- Identify the various personal and professional characteristics that members of Congress possess.

- Examine the member characteristics that you value personally.

- Consider the ways in which members' different personal and professional backgrounds affect their approach to their responsibilities.

Your first assignment as a member of the simulated Congress is to determine which member of Congress you would like to play. When you think about what kind of member you would feel comfortable portraying, you may wish to consider such factors as party affiliation, gender identity, and home state. However, you may not want to choose someone who is just like you or with whom you identify. For example, although portraying a member of Congress who shares your party affiliation might create less internal tension within you, portraying a member of Congress who is not a member of the same political party as you are will give you the experience of exploring the issue positions and motivations of the other party, which in turn may give you greater insights into your own choice of party affiliation. Similarly, although it may be more comfortable to portray a member of Congress who identifies as the same gender as you do, selecting a member whose gender identity is different from yours might provide a unique perspective on the representational issues related to differing descriptive characteristics between members and constituents that confront all members of Congress. Finally, although selecting a member from your home district or home state can be fun because that member's constituents are your friends and neighbors, selecting a member from somewhere else can help you broaden your understanding of the issues confronting other parts of the country.

Choosing a Member

The Member Selection Sheet asks you to select at least three members of Congress that you would be willing to play during the simulation from a list of about 15 percent of the current membership of the 117th Congress. The members available for you to choose have been selected to approximate the demography of the 117th Congress. For each of these members, a committee designator is added to indicate which of five committees the member will serve on in the simulated House of Representatives. The simulated House will have five committees (remember, in reality the House of Representatives at the start of the 117th Congress had twenty standing committees as well as several joint committees and numerous subcommittees). The committees in the simulation are:

Infrastructure The Committee on Infrastructure will consider all legislation that deals specifically with transportation, national resources, and science and technology issues. These issues include, but are not limited to, agriculture, forestry, ecology, energy policy, environmental policy, emerging technologies, highways and public roads, bridges, railways, airline regulation, and air travel.

International Relations/National Security The IR/NS Committee will consider all legislation dealing with bilateral or multilateral relationships between the United States and other countries. It will also consider any legislation dealing with international trade, global markets, espionage, diplomacy, drug trafficking and interdiction, the military, base closures, and immigration.

Health, Education, and Welfare The Health, Education, and Welfare Committee will consider all legislation that deals with health, education, and welfare issues. These issues include, but are not limited to, public health, health care policy, Medicare, Medicaid, pharmaceutical drugs, Social Security, Aid to Families with Dependent Children (and other poverty programs), education policy, teacher testing, national testing standards, and student loans.

Economic Affairs The Economic Affairs Committee will review any piece of legislation that deals with interstate trade, labor issues, consumer protection and consumer affairs, securities and exchange (the stock market, antitrust, monopolies, etc.), work-incentive programs, or other economic issues. This committee will also take on the responsibility of the House Ways and Means Committee, and will be responsible for reviewing legislation referred to it to determine its effects on the U.S. budget. Such legislation would include anything proposing a tax increase or tax cut.

Government and Judiciary The Government and Judiciary Committee will deal with all internal matters relating to the workings or the conduct of government, reforms of the House or other government entities, and rules for members of the legislative branch. Issues such as crime, drugs, abortion, and gun control would also fall under this committee's jurisdiction, as they are policy areas that make up a sizeable part of the actual House Judiciary Committee's jurisdiction. In addition, this committee will deal with any veterans' issues.

In addition to asking you to identify at least three members that you wish to portray, the Member Selection Sheet also asks you whether you want to be a member of the leadership in the simulated House. During the first party caucus, each party will have the responsibility of selecting its leaders and committee chairs from a list of willing students. Members of the majority party will select a majority leader, majority **whip**, and committee chairs for each of the five committees. Members of the minority party will select a minority leader, minority whip, and committee **ranking members** for each of the five committees.

The job of the majority and minority leaders in this simulation, just as in the actual House of Representatives, is to represent their respective parties to the Speaker and before the full House of Representatives. Committee chairs are responsible for maintaining a clear agenda for their committee, including a schedule for hearings and markups. In addition, the chair will be responsible for contacting authors of legislation to inform them of the date/time their legislation will be discussed by the committee and to call them to testify on its behalf, should the committee so desire. The job of the ranking member—the highest-ranking member of the minority party on the committee—is to work with the chair to determine which legislation will be considered, to represent his or her party's interests, and to assist the chair with carrying out any of his or her aforementioned duties. For the most part, the performance of these leadership positions should require only minimal amounts of additional work or time, although these roles will be as strong or as weak as the students serving in them, and the classmates they represent, want them to be.

Please be sure that you carefully and completely fill out the Member Selection Sheet at the end of this chapter. This will help your instructor to assign you and your classmates to members of Congress in a way that maximizes the geographic diversity of the membership as well as tries to approximate the actual demographic composition of the House.

whip This person works for either the majority or the minority party. It is his or her job to ensure party discipline and keep track of members' commitments to vote on a piece of legislation. On party priorities, it is the whip's job to ensure sufficient votes to pass or kill the bill or resolution.

ranking member The highest-ranking member of the minority party serving on a committee.

Where Can I Find Information About Members of Congress?

After this section, you will be able to:

- Identify several of the main primary and secondary sources for information about members of Congress.

- Locate information about the factors that influence members of Congress including their congressional districts and sources of campaign funds.

As you are thinking about which member you want to play or once you have been assigned to play a particular member of Congress in the simulation, it will be essential to seek out information about members of Congress. Information about members of Congress is available from a number of sources. Some of them are more informative and appropriate than others. The following are some potentially useful sources:

- The U.S. Congress online at https://www.house.gov and https://www. senate.gov.
  These are the official websites of the U.S. Congress. From here, you can access the official websites of each member of the House and Senate by following the links to the members' individual sites. On members' sites you will typically find biographical information, statements of their issue positions, and information about their committee assignments. To comply with campaign finance laws, members of Congress maintain separate campaign web pages; you may also find these helpful for understanding the themes and issues important to the member's constituents.

- Members of Congress also maintain social media accounts—usually one set of accounts on Facebook, Twitter, and/or Instagram for their official congressional work and one set of personal or campaign accounts. These accounts can provide quick updates on member activities, and some members use these social media platforms to host virtual events for constituents.

- https://congress.gov. This is the Congress's official online information site. It provides links to substantial amounts of information about members' voting records, their sponsorship of bills and resolutions, and their committee and floor votes, as well as links to additional internet and textual sources of information about members, their legislation, and the legislative process more generally. You can also search the *Congressional Record* for transcripts of floor debate in both chambers.

- The U.S. Census Bureau's "My Congressional District" Tool. Available online at https://www.census.gov/mycd/. The U.S. Census makes congressional district-level data available. Information available includes demographic, employment sector, educational attainment, housing, and other data collected by the U.S. Census Bureau.

- *Congress at Your Fingertips* (Washington, D.C.: CQ/Roll Call, 2021). A handheld quick guide to the members, staff, and committees in the Congress.

- Molly Reynolds, *Vital Statistics on Congress.* (Washington, D.C.: Brookings Institution 2021). A series of statistics covering everything from members of Congress to legislative outputs to staffing levels. Available online at https://www.brookings.edu/multi-chapter-report/vital-statistics-on-congress/.

- OpenSecrets.org. A project of the Center for Responsive Politics, OpenSecrets.org makes federal campaign finance data available for all congressional candidates. Available online at https://www.opensecrets.org/.

Simulation Assignment 2: Member Biosketch

In this assignment you will:

- Identify the ways in which members' of Congress's personal characteristics are similar to or different from their district's demographics.

- Trace the electoral history of a member of Congress.

- Examine the personal, professional, and district influences that affect members of Congress's representational and legislative behaviors.

- Distinguish among the ways in which members of Congress present themselves to their constituents, their colleagues, and during media and fundraising events.

Once you know which member of the U.S. House of Representatives, you'll be portraying, your first task is to draft a biosketch of yourself as a member of Congress. Members of Congress curate their images and are careful about the information they present to the public. This assignment asks you to draft the member's biosketch that might appear on an official congressional website or on the member's campaign site, or that would be used to introduce the member to an audience at a fundraiser or media event. The biosketch should be written as if the members themselves actually did the writing (so, it should be written in the first person: "I am a member of Congress from the second district…," etc.). A thorough biosketch includes most of the following information:

- The member's personal background (age, race, gender identity, religious background, education, occupation, legislative style).
- The location, size, and population demographics of the member's congressional district.
- The main industry or enterprise within the member's district, if any.
- The member's primary concerns, issue positions, and examples of any important legislative successes.
- The length of time the member has been in Congress.
- The electoral circumstances of the last election (won with large majority, won with small majority, beat an incumbent, etc.).
- Any additional information that provides insight into your member of **Congress**.

To assist you with crafting a biosketch for your member, a worksheet has been included at the end of this chapter. Keep in mind that the more detail you provide, the better able you will be to play the role you have been assigned, and the better you will understand the personal, professional, and district influences on members of Congress. The sources of information about Congress that were described in the preceding text will be helpful to you in composing your member biosketch.

How Members Organize Themselves

After this section, you will be able to:

- Describe the overlapping organizational structures operating within the chambers of Congress.

- Explain the role and function of party caucuses within the chambers of Congress.

- Compare the role and function of committees in Congress with the role played by party caucuses.

One defining feature of the U.S. Congress is the fragmented nature of the institution. Its organizational structure is such that members find themselves accountable to many different individuals. For example, the political parties in the Congress determine the leadership of the chambers, who chairs committees, who sits on the committees, and what the chamber's legislative priorities should be. So, members of Congress must establish positive working relationships with their chamber's party leadership. However, committee chairs have nearly complete autonomy to determine which legislative proposals their committees will hear and act on. Thus, among the organizational structures that members must confront as they attempt to represent the best interests of their constituents, and the best interest of the country, are party caucuses and committees, each of which will be discussed in the following pages.

Party Caucuses

Especially in the House, but in the Senate as well, the political parties are alive and thriving. In fact, the parties represent the most overarching organizational structure in both chambers. The **party caucuses** are important for a number of reasons. First, they provide an opportunity for members to meet alone with their fellow partisans to discuss legislative priorities and legislative strategy. They also provide a forum for the selection of chamber and committee leadership and for the selection of committee members. The leaders of the party caucuses are considered to be the fourth-highest ranking members of the House and Senate leadership. The website of the House Democratic Caucus describes its role as follows:

> The Democratic Caucus works with every Democratic member of the House of Representatives to help achieve consensus, bring their ideas and work to the forefront and ensure members have the tools they need to implement their goals. It is the only subgroup within the House of which every Democrat is a Member. The Caucus nominates and elects the House Democratic Leadership, approves committee assignments, makes Caucus rules, enforces party discipline, and serves as a forum to develop and communicate party policy and legislative priorities. It accomplishes these tasks through weekly Caucus Meetings, on-going Issue Task Forces, the yearly Caucus Issues Conference, periodic special events, and continual Member-to-Member communication.[16]

Although the House Republican Conference (House Republicans call themselves a **conference** rather than a caucus) does not provide a similar description on its website, it performs the same functions for House Republicans as the House Democratic Caucus does for House Democrats.

The Senate caucuses are both similar to and different from the House caucuses. The Senate caucuses (or conferences, as they are also called in that chamber) are similar in that they are responsible for choosing leaders, selecting committee members, and dealing with the general organizational structure of the chamber and the party. However, the Senate conferences differ from their House counterparts in that each Senate Conference also has a separate Policy Committee, whose job it is to discuss policy priorities and positions for the party. This means that the conferences themselves are service providers for the senators who belong to them, rather than forums for debate and discussion. For example, the Senate Republican Conference website explains that the conference "helps senators communicate their priorities directly to the American people through a wide variety of communications resources, including television, radio, web technology, social media, graphic design, and Spanish language services, among others resources."[17]

party caucus/ conference Organization composed of the members of the chamber from a specific party; used to discuss legislative priorities and legislative strategy as well as to select members of the leadership and of committees. Each party has its own caucus or conference in each chamber.

Simulation Exercise: Party Caucuses

In this exercise you will:

- Consider what qualities make a good leader in the context of the U.S. House of Representatives.

- Collaborate and compromise with others in order to establish goals and priorities.

The first simulation activity, once you have been assigned to portray a member of Congress, is for each political party to assemble its members in a party caucus. Just as in the real House of Representatives, party caucuses are an opportunity for each party to choose its leadership, including the majority and minority leaders as well as committee chairs and ranking members. During the first party caucus, each party will have the responsibility of selecting its leaders and committee chairs. No member may serve in more than one leadership position, and *each of these leadership positions must be filled in order to proceed with the simulation*. Therefore, your instructor may reserve the right to assign students to play these roles if there are not sufficient volunteers.

In addition to choosing leaders, the parties will likely want to discuss what they view as their party-specific priorities. These priorities should be acceptable to most members of the caucus and should reflect the issues that the members of the *simulation* caucus care about. (Please note that these priorities may or may not reflect the priorities of the actual Republican and Democratic parties, although if all students portray their members accurately they will probably not be vastly different.) The caucuses may also want to establish a plan for "opposition research"—that is, for learning about the members in the other party and determining whether any of them are likely to be helpful or harmful to the party's goals.

It is not necessary at this stage for the party to determine precisely what legislation it wants to see passed or what the party's legislative strategy will be. A second party caucus, following the conclusion of committee action on all legislation, will be used for those purposes. That second caucus is described later in this chapter. However, during this initial party caucus, each party might find it helpful to consider what its general party priorities will be and determine which members might be best suited to draft legislation in support of the party's agenda.

Writing Legislation

After this section, you will be able to:

- Assess the factors that influence the nature and content of legislation that members of Congress pursue.

- Identify the major components of multiple types of legislation.

In this section, we turn to the very important task of drafting legislation. Legislation is the vehicle through which changes to public policy are made by Congress. Although rates of bill sponsorship vary, nearly every member of Congress sponsors at least a small number of pieces of legislation—and some sponsor quite a bit. According to GovTrack, the average number of bills introduced by House members during the 116th Congress (2019–20) was approximately 24.[18] Enacting legislation is also a tangible way to demonstrate to constituents that you, as a member, are respected by your congressional colleagues and that you have accomplished something. However, most members of Congress receive substantial amounts of assistance with drafting legislation. This assistance comes in the form of staff help from their personal staffs, their committee staffs, and ultimately, the House and Senate Legislative Counsels' Offices. The **Office of the Legislative Counsel** is "the legislative drafting service" for each chamber.[19]

The Office of the Legislative Counsel for the House of Representatives consists of several dozen staff attorneys, whose job it is to provide "drafting and related assistance to the Members of the House, the House committees, and the conference committees between the House and the Senate."[20] These attorneys are impartial, and their work with members of the House is subject to attorney–client privilege, meaning that their communication with members and their staffs is confidential. Another nonmember source of legislative drafting assistance is interest groups, many of which will circulate drafts of "model" legislation reflecting the group's priorities to congressional offices in which they have a relationship with the member or staff.

Office of the Legislative Counsel The nonpartisan legislative drafting service used by members of Congress and their staffs.

Simulation Assignment 3: Writing Legislation

In this assignment you will:

- Synthesize what you have learned about the types of legislation, influences on members' legislative priorities, and legislator background.

- Develop a novel legislative proposal.

Unfortunately, you do not have a legislative counsel's office at your disposal. Therefore, the drafting of legislation will be exclusively your responsibility. (Some members and staffs do write their own legislation, so this is not entirely out of the realm of real-life circumstances.) To that end, the following guide may be helpful to you. There is also a worksheet at the end of this chapter that will help you to organize your thoughts.

Step 1: Determine the content and type of legislation that you are proposing.

Recall from the previous chapter that in the House of Representatives, there are four major types of legislation: bills, resolutions, joint resolutions, and concurrent resolutions. Each of these was described earlier, but recall that most legislation gets the title "bill" and that there are two kinds of bills—public and private. A resolution is used when the item of legislation is relevant only to the house of the Congress in which it was introduced. Joint resolutions are essentially the same as bills, in that they must be approved in identical form and signed by the president if they are to take effect. Finally, concurrent resolutions are used to express a sense of both houses of Congress, or to make a policy change that affects only the Congress, such as fixing a time for adjournment or creating joint committees within the Congress. Each of these types of legislation will be appropriate under different circumstances, so you will need to have a plan for the subject matter and content of your legislation in order to select the right type.

Once you have determined the type of legislation you are drafting, you will want to indicate it in your legislation, leaving a blank space for the number, as shown on the Legislation Worksheet at the end of this chapter. For the purpose of the simulation, the Speaker will assign each piece of legislation a number, just as legislation is assigned a number in the actual House.

Step 2: Determine on which calendar your legislation should be scheduled.

As if it isn't complicated enough that the House has four different types of legislation (the Senate does too, for that matter), you will recall that the House also has five different calendars. To remind you, these are as follows:

- *Union Calendar.* This calendar is reserved for money bills (i.e., bills that deal with revenues and expenditures, including appropriations bills).
- *House Calendar.* This calendar is reserved for nonmoney bills of major importance. Most substantive measures will be placed on this calendar.
- *Corrections Calendar.* This calendar is used for noncontroversial measures.
- *Private Calendar.* This calendar is used to schedule private bills, discussed previously.
- *Discharge Calendar.* This calendar is used to schedule legislation that has been forced out of committee by a discharge petition. (It is unlikely—although not impossible—that your bill will be scheduled on this calendar. At the time you are drafting your legislation, you should assume that your legislation will be sent to one of the other calendars.)

Step 3: Write the bill.

Now that you have determined the content and type of legislation you're writing and the appropriate calendar for your legislation, the next step is to out what you want it to say.

Step 3a: Write a statement of purpose for the legislation you intend to propose. Some elements are common to all pieces of legislation. For example, every piece of legislation has a statement of purpose that can be found directly beneath its number. This statement of purpose explains what the bill is about. If you look at the sample legislation in Appendix I, you'll notice that these statements of purpose come immediately following the notation "A bill (or joint resolution, etc.) to . . . ," as shown on the Legislation Worksheet.

Step 3b: Make a note on your worksheet as to which type of clause—enacting or resolving—is appropriate. When legislation is drafted, the initial notation of the statement of purpose (which you will notice appears twice on your worksheet) will be followed by either an **enacting clause** or a **resolving clause**. Enacting clauses are appropriate for bills; a resolving clause is appropriate for all types of resolutions. Without these clauses, legislation has no effect. So, every piece of legislation must include the appropriate enacting or resolving clause.

enacting clause The clause at the beginning of bills that triggers the provisions of the legislation to take effect on the bill's passage by the Congress after it is signed by the president.

resolving clause The clause at the beginning of all forms of resolutions that triggers the provisions of the resolution to take effect on its passage by the relevant house or houses of Congress.

Step 3c: Give your legislation a title. In addition to a statement of purpose, most major legislation also includes a title—that is, a way of referring to the legislation. Sometimes these titles are simply descriptive ("Nuclear Threat Reduction Act"); other times, they can be catchy phrases or even can be converted to easy-to-remember acronyms (The Racketeer Influenced and Corrupt Organizations Act becomes RICO). It is said on Capitol Hill that one thing to be careful of is what acronym your title might create. For obvious reasons, an environmentally—friendly member of Congress wouldn't want to introduce anti-dumping legislation with the title "A Ban Against Dumping in Deteriorating Environmental Areas Act"—no one would vote for A BAD IDEA Act. Where it says "Short Title" on your worksheet, fill in the title of your legislation.

Once you have finished with these preliminary steps, it is time to get serious about drafting your legislation. You can find some examples of actual pieces of legislation in Appendix I to help guide your thinking about the format; additional examples of bills and resolutions are available at https://congress.gov.

Step 3d: Draft at least one, but as many as are needed, findings or "whereas" clauses for your legislation. Many pieces of legislation include some justification for the legislation. In the case of bills, this justification, when it is included, usually takes the form of a set or **statement of findings**; it usually comes in the second section of the bill, just after the title. In resolutions, these findings are often presented as **whereas clauses** (see the concurrent resolution in Appendix I for an example). Either way, you will need to present some justification for your legislation.

Both findings and whereas clauses are written as statements of facts—and will often be pieces of information that you identify and cite from expert, outside sources related to the subject of your legislation. However, they are written in slightly different formats. For example, if you were drafting legislation designed to combat climate change, you might include a finding that reads something like: "The U.S. Environmental Protection Agency reports that climate change is happening now (https://www.epa.gov/climate-indicators/)." By comparison, if you were drafting a simple resolution from the U.S. House aimed encouraging greater executive branch action on climate change, you would most likely re-frame the same information as a whereas clause, that might read: "Whereas the U.S. Environmental Protection Agency reports that climate change is happening now…."

statement of findings The justification, often included in bills, for why the legislative proposal is necessary.
whereas clause The justification, often included in resolutions, for why the action the chamber(s) are resolving to take is needed.

Step 3e: Outline the substance of your legislation. The remainder of the legislation should be focused on the substance of what it is you are trying to accomplish. If you are writing a resolution, you will "resolve" to do what it is you want to do. If you are writing a bill, you will simply declare what it is you are doing.

As you write the remainder of the legislation, you will need to separate your main ideas into major headings and include details about each as subheadings, or subsections, as shown on the worksheet. Attach additional sheets as necessary. These details could include the appropriation of funds to support the legislation; they might specify to whom the legislation will apply (the whole country? specific states? specific people?); and/or these details may simply clarify your major themes. It may be easiest for you to think about the rest of the legislation as an outline. You should again refer to the sample pieces of legislation in Appendix I to help guide you through this process.

As you work to draft the substance of your legislation, keep in mind that in order for your colleagues to determine whether to vote in favor of your legislation, they will need to know exactly what it's doing and how much it will cost. Legislation that is vague or unclear is much less likely to be approved. For example, a bill that says as its main substantive provision "community college will be free for everyone" might be appealing at first read to members with community colleges or high numbers of college-bound students in their districts. But that language is not nearly specific enough. In order to make community college free to all, there must be funding to do so—just as most legislative proposals would have costs associated with them. In this example, faculty and staff would still need to be paid and furniture, technology, equipment, and utilities would still be needed in order to provide the education. So if this were your legislative proposal, you would need to decide whether the funds would come from tax increases, cuts to other budget priorities, or some other sources. Then, once funds are identified there must be a mechanism for distributing them to community colleges across the country written into the bill. Will community colleges simply receive an annual allocation from the federal government? Will the funds go directly to students to pay their bills? You will also need to think carefully about the impact of your legislation on other priorities that you or your colleagues care about and write provisions to address any such considerations. In short, you will likely need to spend considerable time drafting and redrafting your proposal. The House Office of Legislative Counsel has a Guide to Legislative Drafting that, although it is written to assist members and staff with crafting legislation, may also be helpful to you. You can find it at https://legcounsel.house.gov/holc-guide-legislative-drafting.[21]

Step 3f: Draft the appropriate sunrise and sunset provisions for your legislation. The last major components of your legislation are appropriate "sunrise" and "sunset" provisions. A **sunrise provision** sets a date for the legislation to take effect. A **sunset provision** sets a date—if you so desire—for the legislation to expire. All legislation includes some form of sunrise provision indicating when it will take effect. This might be in the form of a specific date, a period of time after the legislation is signed into law, or following a particular event or action. Some legislation—especially pilot programs, and certain types of regulations—includes a sunset provision, which also might be in the form of a specific date or might be linked to the expenditure of the funding allocated or the like.

sunrise provision The date on which an item of legislation will take effect.

sunset provision The date on which a law will expire.

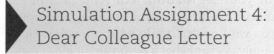

Simulation Assignment 4: Dear Colleague Letter

In this assignment you will:

- Distill complex and specific information from your legislative proposal into a persuasive argument about why your legislation is worthy of support.

- Develop an argument for a non-expert audience about the merits of a legislative proposal.

Once a member of Congress drafts legislation, he or she knows that it will be a long, hard road to passage. In each two-year Congress, thousands of bills and resolutions are introduced. Although the total number of pieces of legislation has declined from the high-water mark of nearly 30,000 during the late 90th and 91st Congresses, the 116th Congress (2019–20) considered more than 16,600 pieces of legislation.[22]

In light of the large number of pieces of legislation, members of Congress use a number of persuasive techniques to convince their colleagues that their legislation ought to be passed. This is not easy; only about 10 percent of all legislation introduced is actually passed by Congress.

Passing legislation can be especially difficult because a member of Congress cannot always count on the full support of his or her political party. While party polarization has increased over the last few decades, partisanship is not the only factor that affects members' voting decisions. In order to reach beyond party lines and raise the interest of as many of their fellow members as possible, many members of Congress use Dear Colleague letters to introduce their legislation to their colleagues, to highlight the need for their legislation, and to set their legislation apart from the (literally) thousands of other pending bills and resolutions.

The format of the Dear Colleague letter is simple. It is almost always a brief, one- or two-page letter from a member of Congress written to fellow members. It introduces the member's proposal, offers some rationale for it, and encourages congressional colleagues to cast a vote in favor. Early on in the legislative process, Dear Colleague letters are frequently used to generate cosponsors for a legislative proposal. Securing both a large number of cosponsors and powerful cosponsors—such as members of the leadership or prominent committee chairs—can be important in setting a legislative proposal apart from the thousands that are introduced in each Congress.

Sometimes multiple cosponsors will sign Dear Colleague letters. (For this initial assignment, you don't have that luxury, although you are welcome to write additional Dear Colleague letters once you have added cosponsors to your legislation.) Two examples of Dear Colleague letters are provided in Appendix II to give you an indication of the appropriate format for such letters.

Simulation Assignment 5: Bill Justification

In this assignment you will:

- Consider the degree to which the legislation you have drafted reflects the priorities and interests of the member of Congress that you are portraying.

- Reflect on the choices you made in crafting your legislation.

In addition to your Dear Colleague letter, it is important for the integrity of the simulation that you spend some time considering why it is that you are proposing your legislation. That is, you need to determine what values you are trying to maximize, what benefits and costs will be incurred by your constituents, and whether you have written a bill that is legitimately within the realm of concern of the member of Congress you have been assigned to portray. For that reason, the next assignment requires that you draft a relatively brief reflective essay about your project, using the guidelines that follow.

Assume that you are writing a letter to a constituent who wants to know why you introduced the legislation you introduced. As any member of Congress would, you should respond to this constituent with a thoughtful explanation of why the bill is important. This response should address different themes from the Dear Colleague letter, although some of the information and/or explanation may overlap. In justifying your legislation, you will likely want to explain to the constituent:

• Why you, as the specific member of Congress whom you are portraying, think that this legislation is important.

• How this legislation is in keeping with your stated legislative goals and priorities.

• How this legislation is consistent with your past activities in the House— or if it is inconsistent, why you believe this inconsistency is rational and justified.

• How this legislation will benefit your constituents—or if it is not directly related to your constituents, why you have chosen to introduce legislation that is more national in scope.

It is important to think through all of these issues to be certain that you are accurately portraying your member, and to ensure that you have a foundation on which to base your arguments in support of your legislation. In other words, this assignment works to ensure that you are being conscious of your member's priorities, not your own, throughout the simulation.

Simulation Assignment 6: Adding Cosponsors

In this assignment you will:

■ Role-play a member of Congress seeking support for his or her legislative proposal in the U.S. House of Representatives.

■ Evaluate others' proposals for their compatibility with your goals and interests.

■ Consider the pros and cons of signing on to other legislation.

cosponsors Additional members of Congress who are willing to put their names on a piece of legislation authored by another member or members.

Once you have drafted your legislation, you will want to seek **cosponsors**— other members of Congress who share your perspective and are willing to put their names on your legislation. In order to do that, you will want to do some research on the voting records of your fellow members to determine whether any of them have previously supported legislation similar to the bill or resolution you have proposed. In addition, you may wish to consider with which interest groups other members have relationships. Interest groups are often involved in the cosponsorship process because they put pressure on members to support particular pieces of legislation. If you believe that one or more of your colleagues should be willing to cosponsor your legislation, you should seek them out and ask them to sign on to your bill.

Cosponsorship generally—although not always—means that you can count on the support of your cosponsor when it comes to debating the legislation in committee or on the floor. It also means that you have leverage over the party leadership, because the more sponsors your bill has, the easier it will be for the leadership to move the legislation once it's on the floor (since there would be fewer people in a position to obstruct the flow of debate on it). Keep in mind that not all legislation has more than one sponsor; some legislation is so particular or specific, or so controversial, that other members are hesitant to support it. Thus, although you will certainly want to try your hardest to find cosponsors, you may not be successful—and that's okay. A cosponsor form is included at the end of this chapter. You can use this form to track your colleagues' commitments to cosponsor your legislation.

While you are seeking cosponsors for your legislation, other members will be seeking you for your support of their proposals. As you consider whether to cosponsor other members' legislation, you may wish to ask yourself the following questions:

- How will this piece of legislation affect my constituents?
- How will this piece of legislation affect the country as a whole?
- How do I (as the member of Congress) personally feel about this?
- How do my fellow party members feel about this legislation?
- Could this legislation be amended to improve it?
- Could this legislation be amended to provide a good or service to my constituents, if one is not already provided?
- How will I explain my vote for or against this legislation?

Committees

After this section, you will be able to:

- Understand the roles that committees play in the U.S. Congress and the ways they vary by committee type and jurisdiction.

- Explain the main steps that congressional committees in the House of Representatives use to process legislation.

Once the caucuses have met to establish the leadership of the simulated House and the individual members of Congress have drafted their legislation, the five committees of the simulation will take control of the legislation assigned to them by the Speaker. Remember that the committees used in this simulation are aggregations of the committees that actually exist in the House of Representatives. This is necessary because trying to run the simulation with 20 committees would not be feasible.

The committees in the simulation, just like the committees in the House of Representatives, are charged with the task of preparing legislative proposals for floor debate. Committees have been called the "workhorses" or the "workshops" of the Congress[23] because so much of the work of members of Congress is done in these committees. Each committee operates differently from every other committee. Some are extremely partisan; in others, members tend to work together across party lines. Some committees, such as the Health, Education, Labor, and Pensions Committee in the House, are constituency focused; others, such as the Foreign Relations Committee in the Senate, rarely consider constituency-based legislation.

During the 117th Congress (2021–22), the Senate had 17 standing full committees and 68 subcommittees. The full committee with the largest number of subcommittees was Appropriations, which alone had 12 subcommittees (essentially one for each of the major appropriations bills) under its jurisdiction. Several Senate committees, including Budget, Indian Affairs, and Veterans' Affairs, have no subcommittees. At the start of the 117th Congress the House of Representatives had twenty full standing committees, with a total of ninety-eight subcommittees.[24] It is at the discretion of the committee chair whether to send items of pending business to a subcommittee or to hold the legislation at the full committee. However, proposed constitutional amendments are nearly always referred to a subcommittee for additional scrutiny. If a subcommittee first considers the legislation, the full committee must still approve it before it can be scheduled on the floor.

Simulation Exercise: Committee Meetings

In this exercise you will:

■ Role-play a member of Congress participating in debate over legislative proposals during a simulated set of committee processes in the U.S. House of Representatives.

■ Evaluate others' proposals for their completeness, clarity, feasibility, and compatibility with individual and collective legislative goals.

■ Engage in small group communication with others to reach consensus about a course of action.

Once bills have been turned in, the Speaker (your instructor) will assign each bill to the appropriate committee or committees of jurisdiction. (Multiple referrals are possible!) The Speaker will make the determination as to which committee is most appropriate based on the descriptions of the five committees provided earlier in this chapter. As a result, your legislation may not end up assigned to the committee that you sit on.

Because of time limitations, it may not be possible for every committee to debate and vote on every piece of legislation during the time set aside in class. In reality, the committees in the House of Representatives and the Senate do not hear, debate, or vote on every proposal sent to them during any given Congress. This is because of the volume of legislation and the time-consuming nature of committee work, because the committee chair has discretion whether or not to hear a piece of legislation, and because some legislation is simply so outlandish that it is not taken seriously. In general, when the committee chair opposes a legislative proposal, it is unusual for it to be given the committee's attention. *It will be at the chair's discretion, in consultation with the ranking member, to determine which legislation to consider or not consider during the simulation, although your instructor/the Speaker may also specify how legislation must be processed.* In general, however, the committees in the simulation should not necessarily feel obligated to hear every piece of legislation referred to them, and indeed they may run out of time before they can consider all the proposals they've been assigned. Committee chairs and ranking members should consider their legislative priorities carefully and use the time set aside for committee meetings productively. Committee chairs and ranking members should also make every effort to assume good faith on the part of their colleagues and should treat each member's legislative proposal with respect, regardless of whether the legislation is ultimately passed out of committee. Remember that when the committees do consider legislation, they generally are sincere in their desire to make improvements to allow the legislation a fair chance on the House or Senate floor. Therefore, committee members in the simulation should also take care to ensure that they are considering legislation fairly. Among the considerations for members should be their party's position on the proposed legislation. But unless one party or the other has a large majority in your simulated House, it will almost always be necessary for the majority party to compromise in order to avoid the possibility that a member or member defects from the party's preferred position for constituency-related reasons.

Committee Meeting #1: Committee Hearings

Once the committee decides to hear your legislation, the committee chair will schedule it for a hearing. As a member of a committee, or when you testify before a committee that is considering your legislation, you should be trying to build support for your legislation; this is the first step toward seeing that your bill has a chance of being voted out of committee. (Here is where being strategic about securing cosponsors may also be helpful to you.) Sometimes you may be called before a committee other than the one you sit on to testify on behalf of your legislation, especially if it was assigned to a committee that you do not sit on. You will simply need to leave your committee meeting and attend the other committee's hearing. This is commonplace in Congress; members of Congress are frequently expected to be in multiple places at once. Remember, if you fail to testify on behalf of your own legislation, it is far less likely to survive committee consideration intact.

Committee Meeting #2: Markup Session

Once the committee has completed its hearings, it will then proceed to a markup session. A markup is similar to the idea of a revision—the committee will literally mark up your legislation with suggested changes to language or content. Members with an interest in the legislation will frequently present amendments to add language to, or delete a passage from, the legislation. During the markup, both substantive language changes and minor technical corrections are made.

Your committee should follow this same model for the markup. You should be prepared to offer amendments to legislation that is troubling to you. In particular, you should seek to amend legislation to provide benefits and services for your constituents, to make the legislation more acceptable to your party, and to ensure that the final product that comes out of committee has a reasonable chance of passage on the floor. Once the bill has been marked up, the committee will take a vote on its passage. If a majority of the committee members support the legislation, it is considered to have been voted out of committee and will be eligible to be scheduled on the floor.

Once a bill is voted out of committee, the proposal's author must be informed by the committee chair of any changes made during the markup. It will then ultimately be the responsibility of the author to draft a final version of the legislative proposal that reflects the committee's changes, and to submit that revised draft to the Speaker with sufficient time for copies to be made and distributed (whether in hard copy or electronically) prior to the full House session. The revised legislation must be accurate; the committee chair and ranking member, who are responsible for managing debate on the legislation that comes out of their committee, will act as a check on the bill's author. However, if electronic copies of the legislation are marked up, the Speaker may request that the committee chair rather than the author keep track of changes to the legislation and be responsible for providing the final, committee-approved version of the legislation to the Speaker. In short, if your legislation is voted out of committee, be sure you know what is expected of you in terms of getting the final proposal ready to be considered during the full House session.

A day or two before the start of floor debate (or before the convening of the Rules Committee, should the Speaker opt to use one), the Speaker will provide each member of the House with copies—either paper or electronic—of all legislation that is to be debated. It is the responsibility of all members of the House to have read all legislation and to be prepared to debate each item of pending business on the floor. If this were the actual U.S. House of Representatives, it would be very difficult for members to be fully prepared for floor debate, as individual pieces of legislation may reach hundreds of pages in length. Of course, members have personal and committee staffs to help them prepare for floor debate, which members of the simulation unfortunately do not have.

The House Rules Committee

In the House of Representatives, as noted in the previous chapter, all legislation that is approved by a committee with jurisdiction over substantive legislative proposals must also be given a rule of debate by the House Rules Committee. These rules determine what sections of the legislation can be amended during floor debate. The House Rules Committee also allows the majority party to control debate because the committee has a supermajority of members of the majority party.

For the simulation, the Speaker (your instructor) can choose one of two options with regard to allowing amendments to legislation during floor debate. First, the Speaker can assign an open rule to all legislation. This means that any section of the legislation being debated on the floor can be amended by any member of the House. The second option is for the Speaker to call on the two parties to create a Rules Committee. A description of this optional activity follows.

Optional Simulation Exercise: Crafting Rules of Debate

In this exercise you will:

- Assess the options available to the House for amending legislative proposals and consider which options are the best course of action in light of individual and collective preferences about legislative outcomes.

- Role-play a member of Congress determining how legislation can, or cannot, be amended by the U.S. House of Representatives.

- Engage in small group communication with others to reach consensus about a course of action.

If the Speaker opts to seat a Rules Committee, the majority party should select four members and the minority party should select two members to serve as the Rules Committee for the simulation. This committee will meet after the standing committees have voted their bills out of committee. It is the job of the Rules Committee to set rules of debate—open, closed, modified, or structured—for each item approved by the committees of jurisdiction. The Rules Committee Worksheet at the end of this chapter contains columns for the bill name or number, the author's name, and the committee of jurisdiction. It also contains columns for the Rules Committee to fill in what rule it is attaching, to explain any rule it decides on, and to record its vote.

During its deliberations concerning which rule it will issue for any item of pending business, the Rules Committee may elect to call witnesses to testify. These witnesses may be the bill's author, the committee chair or ranking member from the committee of jurisdiction, or members of the House leadership. Whether or not the committee elects to call the leaders as witnesses, the members of the Rules Committee should consult with them to ensure that the leadership (especially the leadership of the majority party) is satisfied with the rule that is issued by the committee.

In the event that a Rules Committee is seated, the rules issued by the committee will have to be voted on and approved by the full House session before debate can proceed on the legislation. A Rules Committee tracking worksheet is provided at the end of this chapter to support this simulation element.

Simulation Exercise: Second Party Caucuses

In this exercise you will:

- Role-play a member of Congress participating in a party meeting to craft legislative strategy.
- Set and articulate goals for the party to meet during the upcoming full House session.
- Prioritize the set of legislative proposals available to debate to reflect the goals the party has set for itself.
- Plan for how to use the time available during debate to the party's advantage.
- Engage in small group communication with others to reach consensus about a course of action.

Once your legislation has come out of committee, or out of the Rules Committee if your simulated House opts to use one, it will be necessary for your party to hold a second party caucus. (If your party has been meeting regularly outside of the time set aside for the simulation, then this will be simply the latest in a series of party meetings.) The point here is for your party to refine its priorities by considering which legislation was passed through committee, in order to develop a list of priorities and to forward it to the Speaker (your instructor) so that he or she can determine the order in which the legislation will be scheduled and how much time should be allotted to consider each item. If a Rules Committee was used, the committee may have indicated through its rule a specific number of amendments, and that will need to be taken into consideration during the scheduling process. The Speaker may elect to consult with the Majority Leader and the Minority Leader when setting the agenda for the full House session.

When your party meets in this caucus, it will be important to try to reach agreement on which of the items that came out of committee your party believes should be passed, and which it believes should be blocked or defeated. It will be important to assess whether individual members are uncomfortable with any of the bills supported by the party leadership (the last thing that a party wants is for one of its priorities to be challenged by one of its own members). Your party should also determine which members intend to speak on behalf of, or against, the legislation that is pending and have a plan for how to approach each proposal when it is called up for debate. This will expedite the floor debate process. Finally, in this second caucus, the parties will each want to determine who within their party intends to offer amendments to the legislation, to the extent that the rules adopted permit doing so.

The bottom line is that this party caucus provides a final opportunity for each party to determine its strategy for floor debate. In addition to determining what the party's priorities are, this is a time to determine how best to accomplish those priorities.

Floor Debate and Voting

After this section, you will be able to:

- Outline the major steps of the legislative process in the U.S. House of Representatives.

- Articulate the three options the House has for considering legislation passed out of committee.

Once legislation has been approved by the committee and scheduled by the Speaker, the members' responsibilities shift. Now, members must persuade their colleagues—many of whom know nothing about the legislative proposal—that the legislation is worthy of approval by the full House. You will need to engage in techniques similar to those you used to persuade your committee colleagues to pass your legislation.

Floor debate in the House is both highly regimented and extremely complicated. Walter Oleszek notes that there are six general steps in the floor debate process:

1. Adoption of the rule granted by the Rules Committee.
2. The act of resolving the House into the Committee of the Whole.
3. General debate.
4. The amending process.
5. The motion to recommit.
6. Final action by the full House.[25]

Of course, it is not practical for the simulated House to follow these steps exactly. For one thing, members of Congress do this for a living—that is, they have far more time to spend on these endeavors than do students in a classroom simulation. In addition, the simulated House does not benefit from the presence of the **House Parliamentarian**, whose job it is to advise the Speaker and members—often in real time—about the proper rules of procedure governing the legislative process.[26] Third, the simulation does not allow for motions to recommit

House Parliamentarian A nonpartisan, professional staff member appointed by the Speaker of the House whose job it is to provide advice to members and leaders in the House of Representatives about legislative rules and procedures governing debate in the House.

(a **motion to recommit** is a motion to send the pending business back to the committee that originally approved it for more study or amendments). Therefore, the rules of procedure for debating legislation in the simulation vary somewhat from the rules of procedure used by the actual U.S. House of Representatives. Keep in mind, however, that they serve the same purpose. Just as the rules of debate used by the House of Representatives are designed to create a process conducive to the transaction of legislative business, so too are the rules of procedure for the simulated House.

Although we often refer to floor procedure as occurring in the full House, it's important to note that the House does not often debate legislation acting under the regular rules of debate for the House of Representatives. This is because House rules formally allow for each member to have up to one hour to debate legislation when the House sits as the House—for a total of 440 hours of debate per item of business when all members and nonvoting delegates are included. Instead, for noncontroversial legislation, the House often uses a procedure called the **suspension of the rules**, which limits debate to forty minutes, prohibits amendments, and requires a two-thirds majority for passage. Considering legislation under the suspension of the rules allows the House to quickly act on legislation that enjoys broad agreement.

When legislation is more controversial, the House uses the Committee of the Whole House on the State of the Union (the **Committee of the Whole**) for debate in order to solve the problem of the amount of time that considering legislation in the House itself would consume. In most obvious ways, the Committee of the Whole looks just like the full House—the Committee of the Whole consists of the entire membership of the House, and the Committee of the Whole meets in the House chamber. But by meeting in this "committee," the House can utilize several procedural advantages—including strict time limits on debate such as a five-minute rule (versus a one-hour rule) for the consideration of amendments—in order to expedite the process of considering the legislation. The floor procedures described below governing the full House session in the simulated House likewise take advantage of the time-saving procedures granted by the Committee of the Whole.

Simulation Exercise: Debate and Voting in the Full House Session

In this exercise you will:

- Role-play a member of Congress participating in debate over legislative proposals on the floor of the U.S. House of Representatives.

- Understand the basics of legislative procedure on the floor of the U.S. House of Representatives.

- Use skills of argumentation to reach consensus with others about the proper course of action for multiple legislative proposals.

During the full House session, authors of legislation should be prepared to make a brief statement on behalf of their proposals, and all members of the House should be prepared to participate fully during the debate over their own legislative proposals and those of their colleagues. If your instructor has chosen to incorporate a Rules Committee, then that committee will set the rules of

motion to recommit A motion that, if approved, sends the bill back to the committee of jurisdiction. The motion to recommit is a prerogative of the minority party; it is the minority's last opportunity to revise or kill a piece of pending legislation before the vote for final passage. There are two types of motions to recommit: with instructions or without. A motion to recommit with instructions has the effect of returning the legislation to committee for additional processing in accordance with the instructions; a motion to recommit without instructions has the effect of killing the legislation because it returns the legislation to the committee indefinitely.

suspension of the rules A procedure used to debate and vote on noncontroversial legislation in the House of Representatives. Debate time is limited to forty minutes, the legislation cannot be amended, and a two-thirds majority is required for approval.

Committee of the Whole A time-saving debate procedure in the House of Representatives. Although the Committee of the Whole consists of the entire membership of the House of Representatives, considering legislation in this Committee allows for more flexible and expedited debate than do the rules of the House of Representatives.

debate; it will report each rule in the form of a House resolution that will be debated on and approved separate from the legislation itself. If your instructor does not include a Rules Committee in the simulation, then the Speaker will work with the majority and minority leaders to establish the rules of debate for each piece of legislation. In either case, the House will need to adopt the debate rule before debate can proceed.

In general, floor debate will proceed as follows:

1. The first order of business will be to approve the rule for the first piece of legislation on the agenda. To do so, the majority leader will first need to call up the rule, which should be in the form of a House resolution, before proceeding to debate on the legislation. This is done as follows:

    > Mr./Madam Chair, I call up House Resolution _____, for a period not to exceed _____ minutes, equally divided. For that purpose, I yield _____ minutes to the honorable Minority Leader, and the remainder of my time to the honorable _____, Chairman of the Committee on Rules.

    The minority leader will then respond with:

    > Mr./Madam Chair, I yield my time to the honorable _____, Ranking Minority Member on the Committee.

At this point, the Chair of the Rules Committee would explain the text of the rule and offer the rationale for why it was adopted by the Committee. The Rules Committee's Ranking Member would use her or his time to explain why the minority party either agrees with the rule (in which case, the Ranking Member could simply yield back all time for debate to expedite the process) or why it disagrees. If the minority disagrees with the rule, the Ranking Member of the Committee would explain why and would likely urge the membership to vote down the rule, which also kills the pending legislation it's attached to. *(Note: If multiple rules need to be adopted—e.g., one per item of pending business—the Speaker may elect to vote on all rules before proceeding to the Committee of the Whole. Doing so will expedite floor debate and potentially save time, but note that this approach is different from the procedure used by the actual House of Representatives, which votes on the rule for a piece of legislation immediately prior to debating that piece of legislation.)*

2. Once the rule is adopted, the Speaker will declare the House resolved into the Committee of the Whole (the Speaker then becomes the chair).

3. Once the House has resolved itself into the Committee on the Whole, the majority leader will seek recognition from the chair and call up the proposal associated with the rule, as follows:

    > Mr./Madam Chair, pursuant to House Rules, I call up the _____ proposal to be debated for _____ minutes, equally divided. For that purpose, I yield _____ minutes to the distinguished Minority Leader. I further yield the remainder of my time to the honorable _____, Chair of the Committee on _____ [committee of jurisdiction for the bill].

4. The minority leader should respond with:

    > Mr./Madam Chair, I yield my time to the honorable _____, Ranking Minority Member on the Committee.

5. The Committee chair from the committee of jurisdiction will say:

> I thank the Majority Leader, and recognize _____, the author of the legislation, for a period of one minute to explain the proposal.

Note: This time does not count against the majority.

6. The bill/resolution's author now summarizes his or her legislation. During this time, the author should offer any changes to his or her bill. These are considered to be technical corrections and thus will be considered as part of the original bill.

7. Once the author has summarized his or her bill, the chair announces: "We will now move into a period of general debate." At this point, there are a number of options for how to proceed: (1) The majority **floor leader** may debate the measure. (2) The majority floor leader may immediately yield time to another majority member who wishes to debate the measure. If another member debates but does not use all the time allotted to the majority, he or she should yield the remainder of the time back to the majority floor leader, who can then recognize someone else. A combination of options 1 and 2 may also be used.

> **floor leader** On a specific piece of legislation, the person selected from each party to organize the flow of debate. Generally, the majority party's floor leader is the majority leader or the chair of the committee of jurisdiction. The minority party's floor leader is usually the minority leader or the ranking member on the committee of jurisdiction.

Another option is for the majority floor leader to "reserve" his or her time. This means that he or she does not wish to speak on the legislation or that there is no other member who seeks recognition, but that following debate from the minority, the majority floor leader reserves the right to use the time to respond. This is also perfectly acceptable. However, the total amount of time consumed by the majority party for general debate on the measure cannot exceed the amount of time allotted to the majority party by the majority leader.

8. Once the majority party has consumed all of its time or has reserved the remainder of its time, the minority floor leader will be recognized by the chair. The minority party has the same options available to it as did the majority party with regard to floor debate. Again, however, the party cannot consume any time above or beyond what was allotted to it by the majority leader.

9. Debate continues, alternating back and forth between the majority and minority parties, until all time has expired or until there are no more members on either side seeking recognition.

As you think about participating in general debate, you may wish to consider the following tips:

- At any time, a member can rise on a point of "personal privilege" and ask a question of the bill's author. So, if you have a question, you should say: "Mr./Madam Chair, I rise on a point of personal privilege with a question for the author." The chair will recognize you, and you may ask your question. *(Note: This does not subtract from the time allowed for debate.)*

- It is entirely at the discretion of the floor leaders to recognize the floor managers.

- It is entirely at the discretion of the floor managers to recognize members to speak during general debate.

- It is entirely at the discretion of the chair to recognize members to offer amendments.

- Remember: You *are* the member of Congress you are role-playing. So, your positions on legislation should reflect that member's positions. If you are unsure how your member would vote on any given bill, get on the internet, go to the library, call the member's office—whatever you need to do to play your role appropriately.
- This is politics, not personal. *No* personal attacks should be permitted; the chair has discretion on this point.
- Have fun!

Counts Against Time for Debate	Does Not Count Against Time for Debate
Debating the rule	Calling up measures for consideration
Debating the proposal itself	Author's explanation of the pending proposal
Statements made during allocated time	Points of personal privilege

10. Once general debate has concluded on the legislation, if the rule of debate adopted for the proposal allows amendments, the chair will recognize the majority leader, who will state: "Mr./Madam Chair, pursuant to House rules, we will now move into a period of _____ minutes for the purpose of amending this bill. Time shall be equally divided." The chair will then recognize members offering amendments in the order in which amendments were received or the order in which members indicate that they wish to offer an amendment.
    a. The author of the amendment will get one minute to make his or her argument.
    b. The chair will recognize one person to speak against the amendment for one minute.
    c. The amendment will be voted on by the Committee of the Whole.
    d. This process continues until all time has expired, or until all amendments are disposed of.
11. Once the amending process has been completed, the simulated House will set the bill aside. It will not vote on it, as the Committee of the Whole cannot actually approve legislation. All it can do is amend it to make it acceptable. Only the House of Representatives itself can pass legislation.
12. Once debate on all pending business (or as much of it as can reasonably be concluded in the time allotted) is complete, the Committee of the Whole will dissolve itself back into the House of Representatives. According to Oleszek, this is frequently triggered by the rule attached to the legislation that will require the Committee of the Whole to dissolve at that point.[27] In the simulated House, the chair will simply call for a return to the House of Representatives.
13. With the Committee of the Whole dissolved and the House back in session, the House will take up each piece of legislation for a straight up-or-down vote. There will be no opportunities for debate. Instead, the Speaker will simply call up each piece of legislation and ask that a roll-call vote be taken on it.

In order to keep track of what happens to each piece of legislation that is debated, you may wish to use the Bill Tracker Worksheet at the end of this chapter. Keeping track of the fate of each piece of legislation, as well as how you voted on it, may be useful to you as you think about how you will justify your votes to your constituents.

Optional Simulation Activity: Senate Floor Debate

In this exercise you will:

- Role-play a senator participating in debate over legislative proposals that have been approved by the U.S. House of Representatives.

- Compare the floor procedures used in the U.S. Senate with those used by the U.S. House of Representatives.

- Use skills of argumentation to reach consensus with others about the proper course of action for multiple legislative proposals.

If your class is large enough, or if there is sufficient time, your instructor may wish to refer the legislation that has passed the House to a simulated Senate chamber. Because the focus of the simulation is on the House of Representatives, this optional Senate exercise is not intended to be as extensive as the House simulation. Nonetheless, if used to supplement the House simulation, this exercise can help clarify the differences in procedures used by the House and the Senate.

If your class is small, each student will need to be reassigned to portray a member of the Senate (a list of all of the senators in the 117th Congress is available at http://www.senate.gov). If your class is large enough, some members of the class could portray senators while others portray House members. For this Senate exercise, there are no committees, as the procedures used by Senate committees vary little from those used by committees in the House. The senators should meet in party conferences (which are the same as House caucuses) for the purposes of identifying their legislative priorities; this can be done either inside or outside of class, depending on the timing of this part of the simulation. As part of these conferences, the majority and minority parties should each select a leader and a floor manager for each piece of legislation.

Following these party conferences, floor debate can proceed. Your instructor will serve as the presiding officer, and the majority and minority leaders will manage the floor debate. Unlike the House of Representatives, the Senate has fewer rules of debate. The Senate majority leader will ask that the Senate proceed to its first item of business (whatever piece of legislation the leader wishes to call up first). In order to proceed, the leader will ask unanimous consent to call up the legislation, and for the purposes of the simulation, the assumption will be that there is no objection to the unanimous consent request. Once the legislation is called up, the Senate will move directly into a period of debate on the legislation.

During debate in the actual U.S. Senate, no member of the Senate can speak twice on any single piece of legislation according to Rule XIV of the *Standing Rules of the Senate*. However, Rule XIV does not mention for how long a senator may speak when he or she holds the floor. In fact, in the U.S. Senate, any senator may hold the floor for as long as he or she is able to continue speaking. The *filibuster,* or right of unlimited debate, was once described as permitting a member of the Senate to speak until his knee hit the floor—literally, until the senator fell down from sheer exhaustion. For most of the Senate's history, the chamber had no mechanism to cut off a filibuster. However, in 1917 and again in 1975, the Senate adopted amendments that substantively changed Rule XXII, which is known as the Senate **cloture** rule.[28] The cloture procedure permits 16 senators to petition to end debate. Debate will be brought to a halt if 60 senators (three-fifths of the membership) vote to end debate. If fewer than 60 senators vote to end debate, the filibuster continues, and can only be brought to a halt if the filibusterer(s) decide(s) to give up or if the Senate majority leader "pulls the bill down"—decides to end debate on the legislation. Pulling the bill down is tantamount to an admission by the majority party that it does not have the votes or the clout to ensure passage of the legislation. Calls to change the filibuster process have been growing for nearly a decade, and proposals for reform appear to be gaining steam—it is even possible that the Senate could change these rules while the simulation is underway; your instructor will help you to determine how to proceed if that happens.

In this simulated Senate exercise, just as in the real U.S. Senate, any member of the Senate has the right to filibuster. However, also just as in the real Senate, any senator who engages in a filibuster must be speaking at all times. And, should the other "senators" wish to end debate, they are equally able to use Rule XXII to invoke cloture.

Unlike the House, where the floor managers very actively manage floor debate, in the Senate, debate is managed somewhat by the floor leaders and somewhat by the presiding officer, in large part because of the less regimented nature of Senate debate. The Senate often uses **time agreements**—agreements between the majority and minorities leaders about how long they will permit debate on a piece of legislation. This is similar to the House's use of rules and procedures that require very strict adherence to time constraints.

For this optional exercise, the presiding officer will take on much of the task of managing floor debate. Members seeking recognition should stand and wait to be recognized by the presiding officer (who, again, will be portrayed by your instructor). On being asked by the presiding officer "On what point do you rise?" any member of the simulated Senate may seek to do virtually anything by asking for unanimous consent: "Mr. President, I ask unanimous consent to....." (In the case of the Senate, the presiding officer is referred to as the president, as the official title of the presiding officer is President, or President Pro Tempore, of the Senate.) Debate will continue for as long as members of the Senate continue to seek recognition, provided that the debate conforms to whatever unanimous consent or time agreements the majority and minority party leaders have agreed to ahead of time.

cloture The mechanism for ending a Senate filibuster.

time agreement An agreement between the Senate majority and minority leaders concerning the amount of time that will be spent debating a particular piece of legislation.

Communicating with Constituents

After this section, you will be able to:

■ Describe the ways in which members share information about their Washington activities with their constituents at home.

■ Explain the importance of member communication with constituents.

Once you have concluded the business of debating and approving legislation on Capitol Hill, your focus will shift homeward. As a "single-minded seeker of reelection," an important part of your job is to make what you do in Washington real to your constituents. This is what Richard Fenno Jr. refers to as "home style," or the way that you present yourself to your constituents back home.[29]

Members of Congress have a variety of methods at their disposal for communicating with their constituents. Almost all use their official websites to post information that is relevant to their constituents, and many include information on the sites about projects and services they have procured for their constituents. Many members of Congress make frequent trips home as well to allow them to meet face to face with the residents of their districts. In fact, some members of the House are known as the "Tuesday to Thursday" club because they are only in Washington from Tuesday morning until Thursday night. (The House schedule for voting permits members to keep this sort of schedule.) Some members even sleep in their offices rather than spend the money to rent an apartment or buy a second home.

Of course, members of Congress also take full advantage of their **franking privilege**—their right to send a specified amount of mail using the U.S. Postal Service without having to pay out of pocket for it. They use this privilege to send letters to their constituents in response to constituency requests. Many members also take advantage of the franking privilege to send a periodic newsletter back to their constituents to describe what has taken place on the Hill, and nearly all members use e-mail messages and newsletters to keep their constituents up-to-date on what they are doing in Washington.[30]

franking privilege The right to send a specified amount of mail without paying out of pocket for it. The member's signature, or frank, on the back of the envelope is sufficient to allow the piece of mail to be delivered.

As part of the simulation, you, too, are expected to communicate with the people who sent you to Washington on their behalf. You are to do this by drafting a newsletter to send to your constituents that covers your work in Washington and presents this information in easily understood language and/or visuals.

► Simulation Assignment 7: Constituency Newsletter

In this assignment you will:

■ Synthesize the activities and actions you engaged in during the simulation into a coherent narrative about the work you have done throughout the role-playing experience.

■ Explain your actions to individuals whom you represent but who may lack an awareness of legislative procedure or the ways in which Congress operates.

■ Create clear and informative written and visual materials.

As the session comes to an end, it will be time to turn your attention to reelection. Although it seems like only yesterday that you were campaigning for your seat in this Congress, it's time to start planning to run again. To that end, it's time to communicate with your constituents about your activities during this session of Congress.

Your assignment is to draft a newsletter to your constituents. The newsletter should be of sufficient length to address the following issues:

- Your legislative activities during this session (committee assignments, activities, cosponsorships of legislation, participation in floor debates, etc.).

- Your success/failure to achieve passage for your legislation, and an explanation of the outcome.

- What projects, revenues, and the like you have procured for your district during this session of Congress.

- Information about, and justification for, the bills you supported/did not support in this Congress.

- What you wish had been/had not been enacted.

- **The impact of your work on your constituents.**

As you work on this newsletter, you should consider carefully how best to share information with your constituents. Most word processing programs provide templates that allow you to create a newsletter that includes graphic and visual elements. Today, many members rely on infographics to communicate with their constituents rather than long letters or articles.

In whatever way you decided to share your efforts with your constituents, your newsletter must be clearly written and, as appropriate, visually appealing, free from grammatical and proofreading errors, and must address each of the topics previously mentioned. As you begin to draft your newsletter, you should also keep in mind that you most likely will need to provide some background information on each piece of legislation you mention (since your constituents won't know anything about the legislation except what you tell them). You will also want to be explicit about how your legislative activities will benefit your constituents—remember, this is your opportunity to prove to your constituents that you have served them well.

Chapter Summary

By this point, you have drafted and redrafted legislation, listened to countless proposals from your colleagues, and spent a lot of time considering how to make changes to legislation to adapt and improve it. If the simulation has worked well, you will have discovered the difficulty of drafting legislation, the difficulty of evaluating and amending other members' legislation, and the frustration of seeing your legislation changed. A colleague who went too far in criticizing your legislation may have angered you. You may have felt the anguish of watching helplessly as your colleagues—your friends—ensured that the legislation never saw the light of day. You will likely have felt frustration at the regimented nature of the process, at how thick-headed your colleagues were about the point of your legislation, and at how slow and tedious the legislative process can be. You may be so tired of the Congress that you are simply relieved that the simulation is over.

On the other hand, you may have felt the adrenaline rush that comes from debating your colleagues. You may have felt exhilarated as the legislation you championed passed on the floor of the House or the Senate. You may have felt the satisfaction of seeing the work you did taken seriously by your colleagues. And you may have felt supported by the efforts of your colleagues who agreed with you and worked with you to help you achieve your goals.

If you have these feelings at the end of the simulation, then the simulation worked. You experienced the feelings that real-life members of Congress experience on a daily basis. Most members will tell you that the feelings of satisfaction they get

from serving not only their constituents but also their country are without equal. They typically enjoy bonds of friendship, collegiality, and camaraderie with their fellow members of Congress. They are often hailed as heroes for the legislation they champion that helps to make people's lives better. But members of Congress are also forced to deal with impossible colleagues, difficult legislative proposals, and the time-consuming nature of the legislative process. They must grapple with the competing demands of their constituents, their colleagues, their political party, and their own consciences. Many, especially those who serve in the House of Representatives, maintain two households, and most see very little of their families when the Congress is in session. They endure these difficulties all the while knowing that the institution of the Congress is hated by a large segment of the American public. But in the end, most members of Congress are there because they know that their presence and their hard work do, in most cases, lead to better public policies. They derive tremendous satisfaction from knowing that they are both serving their country and making a difference in people's lives.

Although you did not have to deal with real live constituents, the burdens of balancing a family with life on the Hill, the challenge of supporting two households, the need for constant media attention, or the difficulty of raising money for the next election cycle, you did get a taste of much of the daily activity of a member of Congress. As a result, you have almost certainly also learned a lot about the way the Congress works.

Key Terms

whip 32
ranking member 32
party caucus/conference 35
Office of the Legislative Counsel 37
enacting clause 38
resolving clause 38
statement of findings 39
whereas clause 39
sunrise provision 40
sunset provision 40

cosponsors 42
House parliamentarian 48
motion to recommit 49
suspension of the rules 49
Committee of the Whole 49
floor leader 51
cloture 54
time agreement 54
franking privilege 55

Member Selection Sheet

☐ I DO want to be a member of the leadership

☐ I DO NOT want to be a member of the leadership

Please rank your top three preferences for a member of Congress to portray during the simulation from the following list of members of the 117th Congress. For more information about these members and to help guide your choice, visit their websites, which are accessible at https://www.house.gov. Their committee assignments in the simulated House appear underneath their names, although your instructor may reserve the right to adjust these as necessary to ensure the size and representativeness of each committee in your House of Representatives. Please note that while every effort will be made to assign you to one of your top three choices, there is no guarantee that will be possible. Your instructor may reserve the right to assign you to a different member in order to ensure the partisan and demographic diversity required to approximate the actual U.S. House of Representatives.

Rank	Member
_____	Terri Sewell (D-AL) Economic Affairs
_____	Don Young (R-AK) Infrastructure
_____	Debbie Lesko (R-AZ) Infrastructure
_____	Raul Grijalva (D-AZ) Health, Education, Welfare
_____	Bruce Westerman (R-AR) Infrastructure
_____	Katie Porter (D-CA) Government
_____	Young Kim (R-CA) International Relations/National Security
_____	Jimmy Gomez (D-CA) Government
_____	Michelle Steel (R-CA) Infrastructure
_____	Adam Schiff (D-CA) Government
_____	Mark Takano (D-CA) Health, Education, and Welfare
_____	Ted Lieu (D-CA) International Relations/National Security
_____	Diana DeGette (D-CO) Economic Affairs
_____	Ken Buck (R-CO) Government

Rank	Member
_____	John Larson (D-CT) Economic Affairs
_____	Val Demings (D-FL) Government
_____	Alcee Hastings (D-FL) Government
_____	Charlie Crist (R-FL) Economic Affairs
_____	Brian Mast (R-FL) International Relations/National Security
_____	Mario Diaz-Balart (R-FL) Economic Affairs
_____	Sanford Bishop (D-GA) Economic Affairs
_____	Lucy McBath (D-GA) Health, Education, and Welfare
_____	Austin Scott (R-GA) International Relations/National Security
_____	Kaiali'I Kahele (D-HI) International Relations/National Security
_____	Mike Simpson (R-ID) Economic Affairs
_____	Bobby Rush (D-IL) Infrastructure
_____	Marie Newman (D-IL) Infrastructure
_____	Jan Schakowsky (D-IL) Economic Affairs

Member Selection Sheet (*continued*)

Rank	Member
_____	Adam Kinzinger (R-IL) International Relations/National Security
_____	Trey Hollingsworth (R-IN) Economic Affairs
_____	Randy Feenstra (R-IA) Infrastructure
_____	Sharice Davids (D-KS) Infrastructure
_____	Andy Barr (R-KY) International Relations/National Security
_____	Clay Higgins (R-LA) Government
_____	Chellie Pingree (D-ME) Economic Affairs
_____	Anthony Brown (D-MD) International Relations/National Security
_____	Jamie Raskin (D-MD) Government
_____	Kweisi Mfume (D-MD) Health, Education, and Welfare
_____	Ayanna Pressley (D-MA) Economic Affairs
_____	James McGovern (D-MA) Infrastructure
_____	Peter Meijer (R-MI) International Relations/National Security
_____	Tim Walberg (R-MI) Health, Education, and Welfare
_____	Haley Stevens (D-MI) Health, Education, and Welfare
_____	Jim Hagedorn (R-MN) Infrastructure
_____	Bennie Thompson (D-MS) Government
_____	Cori Bush (D-MO) Government
_____	Jason Smith (R-MO) Economic Affairs
_____	Jeff Fortenberry (R-NE) Economic Affairs
_____	Jerrold Nadler (D-NY) Government
_____	Carolyn Maloney (D-NY) Economic Affairs

Rank	Member
_____	John Katko (R-NY) International Relations/National Security
_____	Adriano Espaillat (D-NY) Health, Education, and Welfare
_____	Elise Stefanik (R-NY) Health, Education, and Welfare
_____	Virginia Foxx (R-NC) Health, Education, and Welfare
_____	Dina Titus (D-NV) Infrastructure
_____	Steve Chabot (R-OH) Government
_____	Marcy Kaptur (D-OH) International Relations/National Security
_____	Tim Ryan (D-OH) Economic Affairs
_____	Michael Turner (R-OH) International Relations/National Security
_____	Markwayne Mullin (R-OK) International Relations/National Security
_____	Earl Blumenauer (D-OR) Economic Affairs
_____	Mary Gay Scanlon (D-PA) Government
_____	Conor Lamb (D-PA) Infrastructure
_____	Fred Keller (R-PA) Health, Education, and Welfare
_____	David Cicilline (D-RI) Government
_____	Joe Wilson (R-SC) Health, Education and Welfare
_____	Scott DesJarlais (R-TN) Infrastructure
_____	Dan Crenshaw (R-TX) Infrastructure
_____	Al Green (D-TX) Economic Affairs
_____	Sheila Jackson Lee (D-TX) Government
_____	Abigail Spanberger (D-VA) International Relations/National Security
_____	Robert (Bobby) Scott (D-VA) Health, Education, and Welfare

Member Biosketch Worksheet

Your Name_____

Member's Name_____

Congressional District_____ State_____

Demographic Profile of the District

_____ Male-identifying (percent)   _____ Female-identifying (percent)

_____ African American (percent)   _____ Asian American/Pacific Is. (percent)

_____ Hispanic/Latinx (percent)   _____ White (percent)

_____ College-educated (percent)   _____ Employed (percent)

Total district population _____

Major corporations, industries, or enterprises, if any

_____   _____

_____   _____

Distinguishing natural or geographic features of the district, if any

_____   _____

_____   _____

Other distinguishing or interesting features of the district

_____   _____

_____   _____

Demographic Characteristics of Member

Member's party affiliation _____

Pre-Congress Career _____

Years of service in Congress _____

Highest level of education _____

Married?   _____ Yes   _____ No

        _____ Number of years

Children?   _____ Yes   _____ No

        _____ Number of children

Member Biosketch Worksheet (*continued*)

Member's Most Recent Election

Percent of the vote won_____

Opponent(s') name(s)

_____   _____

_____   _____

Major campaign themes or promises

_____   _____

_____   _____

Major campaign contributors, including dollar amounts

_____   _____

_____   _____

Member's Policy Priorities

Member's current or previous committee assignments

_____   _____

_____   _____

Member's policy priorities

_____   _____

_____   _____

Members' past legislative achievements

_____   _____

Sources of Information Used in This Assignment

1. _____

2. _____

3. _____

4. _____

Legislation Worksheet

Calendar (Select):   ☐ Union   ☐ House   ☐ Private   ☐ Corrections

117ᵗʰ CONGRESS
☐ 1ˢᵗ ☐ 2ⁿᵈ Session

(Select):   ☐ H.R.   ☐ H. Res.   ☐ H.J. Res.   ☐ H. Con. Res. _____
(leave a blank for the number)

A ☐ Bill ☐ Resolution to

_____

(Explain the purpose of your legislation immediately following the designstor of its type.)

IN THE HOUSE OF REPRESENTATIVES

_____

<u>YOUR MEMBER'S NAME HERE</u> introduced the following bill, which was referred to the Committee on
_____ *(leave a blank--the Speaker will indicate the committee of referral.)*

_____

A ☐ Bill ☐ Resolution to

_____

(Explain the purpose of your legislation again immediately following the designator of its type.)

☐ Be it enacted by the Senate and House of Representatives of the United States of
America in Congress assembled, (This is the enactment clause; you must include this
if you are drafting a bill.)

<u>OR</u>

☐ Resolved by the House of Representatives of the United States of America in
Congress assembled, *(You must include this resolving clause in all resolutions; add
the Senate [as above] if it is a joint or concurrent resolution.)*

SECTION 1. SHORT TITLE

This Act may be cited as _____
(Give your legislation a title here.)

SECTION 2. ☐ FINDINGS OR ☐ WHEREAS CLAUSES
*(In this section, you should give a justification for why this legislation is necessary. Findings are typically used to make a
factual argument about why a <u>bill</u> is needed. Whereas clauses justify the need for a <u>resolution</u>.)*

A. _____
_____
_____

Legislation Worksheet (*continued*)

B. _____
_____
_____

SECTION 3: SUBSTANCE OF THE BILL
(*Indicate here what your legislation is doing. You can use as many subsections as are needed.*)

A. _____
_____
_____

B. _____
_____
_____
_____

C. _____
_____
_____
_____

SECTION 4: DATE OF ENACTMENT
(*Here is where any sunrise clause should be placed.*)

_____
_____
_____
_____

SECTION 5: (optional) EXPIRATION DATE
(*Here is where any sunset clause should be placed.*)

_____
_____
_____
_____

Some Tips for Bill Writing

Here are some general guidelines to keep in mind as you draft your legislation.

- Be as specific as possible.
- Be certain you have addressed potential conflicts and concerns that other members might have.
- Be sure to indicate whether any money should be appropriated and, if so, how much.
- Be sure to indicate how the legislation will be administered. Will it be self-executing, need the states for implementation, or be implemented by federal bureaucratic processes (which ones)?
- Be certain that your legislation reflects your member's goals and priorities, both for the district and for the country.

Cosponsor Form

Legislation Title/Number_____

Sponsored by_____

By signing my name to this form, I agree to cosponsor the legislation named above.

Student Name   Member Name   Signature

_____

_____

_____

_____

_____

_____

_____

_____

_____

_____

_____

_____

_____

Rules Committee Tracking Worksheet

Legislation Name / Number	Author	Rule Type	Specific terms of the rule, if any?
		Open Closed Modified Structured	
		Open Closed Modified Structured	
		Open Closed Modified Structured	
		Open Closed Modified Structured	
		Open Closed Modified Structured	
		Open Closed Modified Structured	
		Open Closed Modified Structured	

Bill Tracker Worksheet

Bill Title/Number	Author	Yea Votes (in favor)	Nay Votes (against)	My Vote (yea or nay)

4

Resources for Future Study

Learning Objectives

After this chapter, you will be able to:

- Describe the scope of existing scholarship related to the U.S. Congress.

- Identify useful resources to assist you with learning more about the U.S. Congress.

Literally thousands of books and articles have been written about the U.S. Congress. These range from texts that describe the legislative process to biographies of members of Congress to historical treatments of the institution to discussions of particular legislative proposals that have been debated and approved by the Congress. For students confronted with the need to conduct research on the process, they can be daunted by the task of sifting through all of these texts. The annotated bibliography that follows is an attempt to make students aware of a tiny fraction of the resources available. It should not be treated as a comprehensive listing of all the resources that exist.

Recent Articles

Brant, Hanna K., and L. Marvin Overby. "Congressional Career Decisions in the 2018 Congressional Midterm Elections," *Congress & the Presidency* **48, no. 1 (2021): 8–24.** Retirements are more responsible for turnover in congressional seats than are elections. In this article, Brant and Overby explore U.S. Congress members' motivations for deciding not to seek reelection.

Chaturvedi, Neilan. "Filling the Amendment Tree: Majority Party Control, Procedures, and Polarization in the U.S. Senate," *American Politics Research* **46, no. 4 (2018): 724–47.** Senators have complained for decades that chamber majority leaders have limited their ability to offer amendments by "filing the amendment tree," that is, consuming all the possible amendment spots themselves. Chaturvedi finds that rank-and-file senators of the majority party were not precluded from offering amendments, but that filing the amendment tree did have consequences for senators' voting behavior.

Craig, Allison W. "It Takes a Coalition: The Community Impacts of Collaboration," *Legislative Studies Quarterly* 46 (2021): 11–48. Craig's study of more than 30,000 "Dear Colleague" letters finds that members of Congress who have more "social influence"—that is, greater connection with their colleagues as measured through co-signing Dear Colleague letters—are able to secure greater benefits for the constituents.

Crosson, Jesse M., Alexander C. Furnas, Timothy Lapira, and Casey Burgat. "Partisan Competition and the Decline in Legislative Capacity among Congressional Offices." *Legislative Studies Quarterly* (2020). Early view doi:10.1111/lsq.12301. Using a dataset of payroll disbursements, the authors find that members of Congress from both parties have been committing declining resources to compensating legislative staff, instead shifting a greater share of their resources to constituency service and public relations staff members.

Lawless, Jennifer, Sean M. Theriault, and Samantha Guthrie. "Nice Girls? Sex, Collegiality, and Bipartisan Cooperation in the US Congress," *The Journal of Politics* 80, no. 4 (2018): 1268–82. Lawless, Theriault, and Guthrie set out to explore whether the gendered assessments of female-identifying members of Congress who accomplish policy goals as cooperative and collaborative reflect the reality of the ways in which these legislators engage with their colleagues. They find little to indicate that women members behave different from their male-identifying colleagues on a variety of forms of congressional work.

Park, Ju Yeon. "When Do Politicians Grandstand? Measuring Message Politics in Committee Hearings." *The Journal of Politics* (March 27, 2020). Although congressional hearings are thought to be about processing legislation and sharing important legislative information with the full chamber, Park finds that hearings are also used for "grandstanding" activities—those that are aimed at framing or sending a political message. This article reports on efforts to develop a grandstanding score and to determine which members engage in grandstanding, and under what conditions.

Ritchie, Miranda N., and Hye Young You. "Legislators as Lobbyists," *Legislative Studies Quarterly* 44 (2019): 65–95. In this article, Ritchie and You document the many ways that members of Congress engage in constituency service, including direct lobbying of the executive bureaucracy to make decisions that will benefit the member's constituents. Moreover, based on thousands of communications obtained via Freedom of Information Act Requests, the authors find that when lobbyists appeal to bureaucrats' discretion, they are often successful.

Books

Biographies/Autobiographies of Members of Congress

Boehner, John. *On the House: A Washington Memoir.* New York: St. Martin's Press, 2021. Boehner—who served as Speaker of the U.S. House of Representatives under both President George W. Bush and President Barack Obama—reveals the eye-opening reality of life and work as a Washington D.C., insider in his long-awaited 2021 autobiography.

Brown, Sherrod. *Desk 88: Eight Progressive Senators Who Changed America.* **London: Picador Press, 2020.** Brown, a senator from Ohio, sits at Desk 88 in the chamber, and uses this text to tell not only his own story and offer his own vision for governing, but also to tell the stories of eight of his predecessors who were assigned to Desk 88, including such prominent members of the chamber as Hugo Black, who would later be appointed to the U.S. Supreme Court by President Franklin D. Roosevelt.

Caro, Robert A. *The Years of Lyndon Johnson, Master of the Senate.* **New York: Alfred A. Knopf, 2002.** This is volume three of Caro's four-volume series (so far) covering the life and career of Lyndon Johnson. In this volume, Caro turns his attention to Johnson's years as a U.S. Senator and, later, Senate Majority Leader, from Texas. Caro demonstrates the skillful way that Johnson used his personal political strengths to augment the limited power available to Senate leaders and accomplish his policy objectives.

Dingell, John D., and David Bender. *The Dean: The Best Seat in the House.* **New York: HarperCollins Publishers, 2018.** Dingell was the longest-serving member of the U.S. House of Representatives in history, serving a total of 59 years from 1955 to 2015. In this memoir, he offers personal perspectives on the ways in which Congress and American politics changed over this period of time, and ultimately, offers a defense of the possibilities of government to serve the common good.

McCain, John, and Mark Salter. *The Restless Wave: Good Times, Just Causes, Great Fights, and Other Appreciations.* **New York: Simon & Schuster, 2019.** McCain's memoir, written following his diagnosis of terminal cancer, is a candid review of his years as a Senator, his 2008 campaign for the presidency, and his political interests in international relations and diplomacy. Like other long-serving members of Congress, McCain decries the loss of collegiality and the rise of partisanship.

McConnell, Mitch. The Long Game: A Memoir. London: Penguin Books, 2019. McConnell spent six years as Senate Majority Leader (2015–21) during a period that spanned the second term of President Barack Obama and the election and presidency of President Donald Trump. McConnell's memoir describes his upbringing and political career, and offers observations about the state of American politics from a long-time participant in politics known for his keen, and sometimes ruthless, political acumen.

Ornstein, Norman J. *Lessons and Legacies: Farewell Addresses from the Senate.* **Reading, MA: Addison Wesley, 1997.** In 1996, thirteen U.S. senators voluntarily retired from the chamber—the most ever in modern history. In this volume, the American Enterprise Institute's Ornstein shares their thirteen farewell addresses from the Senate floor. Although each is different from the others, the retiring senators collectively lament an institution beset by partisanship and losing its way as the world's greatest deliberative body—trends that have only continued to accelerate since then.

Page, Susan. *Madam Speaker: Nancy Pelosi and the Lessons of Power.* **New York: Hachette Book Group, 2021.** This biography by the Washington, D.C., bureau chief of *USA Today* newspaper details the origins and ascendency of the first woman Speaker of the U.S. House of Representatives, Nancy Pelosi, from her upbringing through the Trump administration and her many years serving as the highest-ranking woman in U.S. politics (until Vice President Kamala Harris was sworn in on January 20, 2021).

Rogers, Mary Beth. *Barbara Jordan: American Hero.* **New York: Bantam Doubleday Dell, 2000.** Jordan was a civil rights leader who broke both racial and gender barriers in the 1960s and 1970s. After being elected as the first African American member of the Texas senate since Reconstruction in 1966, Jordan became the first African-American woman elected to the U.S. House of Representatives from the South in 1972.

Warren, Elizabeth. *Persist.* **New York: Henry Holt & Company, 2021.** Mixing personal memoir with real-life experiences as a member of the U.S. Senate, Massachusetts Senator Warren offers her perspectives on contemporary politics and calls on readers to engage in the political process themselves.

How Congress Works

Baker, Ross K. *House and Senate,* **4th ed. New York: W.W. Norton, 2008.** Baker relies on interviews with current and former members of Congress, including senators who previously served in the House of Representatives as well as congressional staff members, lobbyists, and others with first-hand knowledge of the two chambers to describe the ways in which the U.S. House and Senate work together—and don't.

Congressional Quarterly. *American Congressional Dictionary.* **Washington, D.C.: Congressional Quarterly Press, 2001.** This text—literally a dictionary of important congressional terms—serves as an important decoder for the specific terms and concepts that describe the legislative process and congressional activities.

Fenno Jr., Richard F. *Homestyle: House Members in Their Districts.* **London: Pearson/Longman, 2002.** In this classic work, political scientist Richard Fenno follows multiple members of Congress into their districts to study their interactions with their constituents and the ways in which they present their Washington, D.C., activities to those they've been sent there to represent.

Grimmer, Justin. *Representational Style in Congress: What Legislators Say and Why It Matters.* **Cambridge, UK: Cambridge University Press, 2013.** No matter how hard members of Congress work to represent their constituents, it means little if members' constituents don't know what their members are doing. Using a comprehensive dataset of U.S. Senate press releases from 2005–2007, Grimmer shows that senators adopt a variety of presentational styles to translate their work in Congress back to their constituents at home, and that these styles are likewise influenced by a variety of constituency characteristics.

Grose, Christian R. *Congress in Black and White: Race and Representation in Washington and at Home.* **Cambridge, UK: Cambridge University Press, 2011.** This study, undertaken in the wake of Barack Obama's historic election in 2008, asks whether electing Black representatives matters to the representation of Black interests. While Grose finds that it does, in exploring this question, he reveals the complexity of such interests and demonstrates that traditional political science explanations for the reasons members of Congress behave the way they do are insufficient to understanding the ways in which Black descriptive and substantive representation intersect.

LaPira, Timothy M., Lee Drutman, and Kevin R. Kosar, eds. *Congress Overwhelmed: The Decline in Congressional Capacity and Prospects for Reform.* **Chicago: University of Chicago Press, 2020.** In this edited volume, LaPira, Drutman, and Kosar bring together prominent congressional scholars who describe and analyze the ways that Congress's systematic reduction of its own information and financial resources has left it ill-equipped to serve as a meaningful counterweight to the executive branch of government. The consequence is that Congress can no longer adequately fulfill many of the functions required of it in our constitutional order.

Price, David E. *The Congressional Experience,* **4th ed. Milton Park, UK: Routledge, 2020.** One of only a handful of political scientists to serve in Congress, Price is able to link academic approaches to the study of Congress with the practical realities of actually serving in the U.S. House of Representatives. He chronicles the ways in which legislative procedures have changed over time and offers a current and relevant look at the ways in which the Trump impeachment and COVID-19 global pandemic affected the U.S. House.

Congress and the Legislative Process

Binder, Sarah A., and Stephen S. Smith. *Politics or Principle: Filibustering in the United States Senate.* **Washington, D.C.: Brookings Institution Press, 1997.** Binder and Smith's 1997 book was the first comprehensive exploration of filibustering activity in the U.S. Senate. This book continues to shed light on the Senate's defining procedure at a time when the filibuster has come to represent everything that is wrong with the U.S. Congress.

Mayhew, David R. *Congress: The Electoral Connection,* **2nd ed. New Haven: Yale University Press, 2004.** David Mayhew is one of the most prominent scholars of the U.S. Congress, and *Congress: The Electoral Connection* is one of his most important works. Mayhew tells us that members of Congress are "single-minded seekers of reelection," and demonstrates that so much of the ways in which members behave can be explained by knowing this one piece of information about what motivates them.

Oleszek, Walter J., Mark J. Oleszek, Elizabeth Rybicki, and Bill Heniff Jr. *Congressional Procedures and the Policy Process,* **11th ed. Washington, D.C.: Congressional Quarterly Press, 2019.** The latest edition of Congressional Research Service (CRS) veteran Walter J. Oleszek's primer on legislative procedures features the addition of three new coauthors, all of whom are staff members for CRS as well. This is an essential text for understanding both basic, and more nuanced, elements of House and Senate legislative procedures.

Redman, Eric. *The Dance of Legislation: An Insider's Account of the Workings of the United States Senate.* **Seattle: University of Washington Press, 2001.** Redman first published this first-hand account of the intricacies of the legislative process in 1973, following two years of work as a Senate staffer on the National Health Service bill. Although many of the details of the legislative process have changed in the nearly five decades since Redman published his initial account, he reveals the extent to which that even historically, the passage of legislation in the U.S. Senate (and Congress, more generally) has required the navigation of a complicated labyrinth of procedural, personal, and political considerations.

Rosenthal, Cindy Simon. *Women Transforming Congress.* Norman, OK: University of Oklahoma Press, 2003. In this edited volume, a diverse group of scholars tackle questions relating to women's participation in the U.S. national legislature. The volume considers changing gender demographics, women's impact on institutional processes, and the effect of women on various public policy areas.

Sinclair, Barbara. *Unorthodox Lawmaking: New Legislative Processes in the U.S. Congress,* 5th ed. Washington, D.C.: Congressional Quarterly Press, 2016. Sinclair was among the first congressional scholars to document the ways in which the House and Senate were abandoning "regular order" for special legislative processes that strengthened parties and leaders while reducing the capacity of Congress as an institution and undermining the predictability of the legislative process in Congress.

Swers, Michele. *The Difference Women Make: The Policy Impact of Women in Congress.* Chicago: University of Chicago Press, 2002. *The Difference Women Make* was the first comprehensive treatment of the ways that female-identifying and male-identifying representatives engage in the policymaking process and the ways in which differences along gender lines influence policy outcomes in Congress.

Tyson, Vanessa C. *Twists of Fate: Multiracial Coalitions and Minority Representation in the US House of Representatives.* Oxford, UK: Oxford University Press, 2016. In this text, Tyson provides an important perspective on the ways in which members of the U.S. House of Representatives from historically underrepresented groups find each other and build cross-racial coalitions with one another, often to advance a legislative agenda supportive of marginalized groups and social justice.

Helpful Websites

Congress's Main Website: https://www.congress.gov. Find comprehensive links to legislation introduced in the current and previous congresses, as well as links to the *Congressional Record,* Congressional Research Service reports, chamber websites, member websites, leadership websites, and a range of learning tools about the national legislature.

The Library of Congress: https://www.loc.gov. Search the collections held by the Library of Congress on this website, which also offers links to a variety of online research materials and exhibitions that may be useful as you explore important public issues and problems.

The U.S. House of Representatives: https://www.house.gov. Here, you can find information specific to the U.S. House, including member websites, committee websites, links to votes cast, and schedules for upcoming hearings and floor debates.

The U.S. Senate: https://www.senate.gov. Here, you can find information specific to the U.S. Senate, including member websites, committee websites, links to votes cast, and schedules for upcoming hearings and floor debates. In addition, there are robust links to stories about Senate history and that explain the art and architecture of the Senate building.

Notes

Chapter 1

1. George Galloway, *History of the United States House of Representatives* (Washington, D.C.: Government Printing Office, 1965).

2. Frances E. Lee and Bruce I. Oppenheimer, *Sizing Up the Senate: The Unequal Consequences of Equal Representation* (Chicago: University of Chicago Press, 1999).

3. Jan Ellen Lewis, "What Happened to the Three-Fifths Clause: The Relationship between Women and Slaves in Constitutional Thought, 1787–1866," *Journal of the Early Republic* 37, no. 1 (2017): 1–46.

4. Janai Nelson, "Counting Change: Ensuring an Inclusive Census for Communities of Color," *Columbia Law Review* 119, no. 5 (2019): 1399–1448.

5. Ashley English, Kathryn Pearson, and Dara Strolovitch, "Who Represents Me? Race, Gender, Partisan Congruence, and Representational Alternatives in a Polarized America," *Political Research Quarterly* 72, no. 4 (2019): 785–804.

6. Ross K. Baker, *House and Senate*, 3d ed. (New York: W.W. Norton, 2001), 38–9.

7. James Sterling Young, *The Washington Community* 1800–1828 (New Haven, CT.: Yale University Press, 1966).

8. Ibid.

9. Ibid.

10. Young, 13.

11. Ida Brudnick, "Salaries of Members of Congress: Recent Actions and Historical Tables," *CRS Report for Congress* (Washington, D.C.: Library of Congress, 2021).

12. Members' biographies can be found online at https://bioguide.congress .gov/; the guide is a joint effort of the House and Senate Historians' and Clerks' offices.

13. Donald Matthews, *U.S. Senators and Their World* (New York: W.W. Norton, 1973).

14. Brian Alexander, *A Social Theory of Congress: Legislative Norms in the Twenty-First Century* (Washington, D.C.: Lexington Books, 2021).

15. Ida Brudnick, "Congressional Salaries and Allowances: In Brief," *CRS Report for Congress* (Washington, D.C.: Library of Congress, 2018).

16. Robert H. Salisbury and Kenneth A. Shepsle, "Congressman as Enterprise," *Legislative Studies Quarterly* 6 (1981): 559–76.

Chapter 2

1. Barbara Sinclair, *Unorthodox Lawmaking, 5th ed.* (Washington, D.C.: Sage/CQ Press, 2016).

2. *Standing Rules of the Senate* (Washington, D.C.: Government Printing Office, 1990).

3. Walter J. Oleszek, *Congressional Procedures and the Policy Process*, 4th ed. (Washington, D.C.: Congressional Quarterly Press, 2001), 339–40.

4. Michael D. Minta and Nadia E. Brown, "Intersecting Interests: Gender, Race, and Congressional Attention to Women's Issues," *Du Bois Review* 11, no. 2 (2014): 254.

5. Christopher Witko, Jana Morgan, Nathan J. Kelly, and Peter K. Enns, *Hijacking the Agenda: Economic Power and Political Influence* (New York: Russell Sage Foundation, 2021).

6. Valerie Heitshusen, "Introduction to the Legislative Process in the U.S. Congress," *CRS Report for Congress* (Washington, D.C.: The Library of Congress, 2020).

7. Christopher J. Deering and Steven S. Smith, *Committees in Congress*, 3d ed. (Washington, D.C.: Congressional Quarterly Press, 1997), 11–12.

8. Christopher M. Davis, "The Legislative Process on the House Floor: An Introduction," *CRS Report for Congress* (Washington, D.C.: The Library of Congress, 2019).

9. Donald Wolfensberger, "House Rules Data," available from the Bipartisan Policy Center online, last accessed March 5, 2021, https://bipartisanpolicy.org/report/house-rules-data/.

10. Oleszek, 157.

11. House Rule XIII.

12. Oleszek, 112.

13. Mary E. Mulvihill, Paul Rundquist, Judy Schneider, and Lorraine H. Tong, "House and Senate Rules of Procedure: A Comparison," *CRS Report for Congress* (Washington, D.C.: Library of Congress, April 7, 1999), 3.;

14. Mulvihill et al., 3.

15. Mulvihill et al., 5.

16. Sinclair, 93.

17. Sinclair, 90.

18. Gary W. Cox and Mathew D. McCubbins, *Setting the Agenda: Responsible Party Government in the U.S. House of Representatives* (Cambridge: Cambridge University Press, 2005).

19. Frances E. Lee, "Agreeing to Disagree: Agenda Content and Senate Partisanship, 1981–2004," *Legislative Studies Quarterly* 33, no. 2 (2008): 199–222.

20. Sinclair, 19.

21. James Curry, *Legislating in the Dark* (Chicago: University of Chicago Press, 2018), 3.

22. John D. Rackey and Lauren C. Bell, "The Incredible Shrinking Witness List: Information Loss in Congress," unpublished manuscript, 2021.

23. Abby Vesoulis, "'He's Saying One Thing and Then He's Doing Another': Rep. Madison Cawthorn Peddles a Different Kind of Trumpism in a Post-Trump World," *Time*, 2021, last accessed March 7, 2021, https://time.com/5931815/madison-cawthorn-post-trump/.

24. Sarah Binder, "A Primer on Self-Executing Rules," Brookings Institution Online, 2010, last accessed March 7, 2021, https://www.brookings.edu/blog/up-front/2010/03/17/a-primer-on-self-executing-rules/.

25. See GovTrack.us, "Statistics and Historical Comparisons," 2021, last accessed March 6, 2021, https://www.govtrack.us/congress/bills/statistics.

26. Anonymous, "Outrageous Bills," *The Economist* 409, no. 8863 (November 23, 2013): 32.

27. Sinclair, 71.

28. Glen S. Krutz, *Hitching a Ride: Omnibus Legislating in the U.S. Congress* (Columbus: Ohio State University Press, 2001).

29. John Hudak, *Presidential Pork: White House Influence over the Distribution of Federal Grants* (Washington, D.C.: Brookings Institution Press, 2014).

30. Jennifer Shutt, "House Appropriators Officially Bring Back Earmarks, Ending Ban," RollCall.com, 2021, last accessed March 6, 2021, https://www.rollcall.com/2021/02/26/house-appropriators-to-cap-earmarks-at-1-percent-of-topline/.

31. Carly Schmitt and Hanna K. Brant, "Gender, Ambition, and Legislative Behavior in the United States House," *Journal of Women, Politics & Policy* 40, no. 2 (2019): 286–308.

32. Sara Angevine, "Representing All Women: An Analysis of Congress, Foreign Policy, and the Boundaries of Women's Surrogate Representation," *Political Research Quarterly* 70, no. 1 (2017): 107.

33. See, last accessed March 7, 2021, https://www.govtrack.us/congress/votes/89-1965/h87.

34. See, last accessed March 7, 2021, https://www.congress.gov/bill/117th-congress/house-bill/1.

35. Chris Riotta, "GOP Aims to Kill Obamacare Yet Again after Failing 70 Times," *Newsweek* (online), 2017, last accessed March 7, 2021, https://www.newsweek.com/gop-health-care-bill-repeal-and-replace-70-failed-attempts-.

36. Logan Dancey and Geoffrey Sheagley, "Partisanship and Perceptions of Party-Line Voting in Congress," *Political Research Quarterly* 71, no. 1 (2018): 32.

37. Ezra Klein, "The Most Depressing Graphic for Members of Congress," *Washington Post*, January 14, 2013, last accessed March 6, 2021, https://www.washingtonpost.com/news/wonk/wp/2013/01/14/the-most-depressing-graphic-for-members-of-congress/.

38. Karl Evers-Hillstrom, "State of Money in Politics: The Price of Winning Is Steep," OpenSecrets.org, 2019, last accessed March 7, 2021, https://www.opensecrets.org/news/2019/02/state-of-money-in-politics-the-price-of-victory-is-steep/.

39. Colleen J. Shogan, "Blackberries, Tweets, and YouTube: Technology and the Future of Communicating with Congress," *PS: Political Science and Politics* 43, no. 2 (2010): 231–33.

40. U.S. Census, "New York Congressional District 14—Representative Alexandria Ocasio-Cortez," 2019, available online at https://www2.census.gov/geo/maps/cong_dist/cd116/cd_based/ST36/CD116_NY14.pdf, last accessed March 6, 2021.

Chapter 3

1. David Mayhew, *Congress: The Electoral Connection* (New Haven, CT: Yale University Press, 1974).

2. Linda L. Fowler, "Who Runs for Congress?" *PS: Political Science & Politics* 29, no. 3 (Washington, D.C.: American Political Science Association, 1996).

3. Gary C. Jacobson and Samuel Kernell, "Strategic Politicians" (excerpt from *Strategy and Choice in Congressional Elections*, 2nd ed., 1983), in *Classics in Congressional Politics*, eds. Herbert F. Weisberg, Eric S. Heberlig, and Lisa M. Campoli (New York: Addison, Wesley, Longman, 1999).

4. Thomas A. Kazee, ed., *Who Runs for Congress: Ambition, Context, and Candidate Emergence* (Washington, D.C.: Congressional Quarterly Press, 1994), 175.

5. Richard F. Fenno Jr., *Home Style: House Members in their Districts* (Glenview, IL: Scott Foresman, 1978); John R. Hibbing, *Congressional Careers: Contours of Life in the U.S. House of Representatives* (Chapel Hill: University of North Carolina Press, 1991).

6. Kazee, 175.

7. David Faris, "Matt Gaetz and the Tyranny of the Backbencher," *The Week*, April 5, 2021, last accessed April 10, 2021, https://theweek.com/articles/975660/matt-gaetz-tyranny-backbencher.

8. Eric Hansen and Sarah Treul, "Inexperience or Anti-Washington: Voter Preferences for Congressional Candidates," Working Paper, 2019, last accessed April 10, 2021, http://ehansen4.sites.luc.edu/documents/Hansen_Treul_MPSA_2019.pdf.

9. Jennifer Manning, "Membership of the 117th Congress: A Profile," *CRS Report for Congress* (Washington, D.C.: Congressional Research Service, March 17, 2021), 1.

10. See https://ourworldindata.org/gender-ratio for longitudinal data on the proportion of men and women in the U.S. population.

11. Manning, 1.

12. Ibid., 2.

13. Ibid., 3.

14. Ibid., 3, 9.

15. Ibid., 4–5.

16. U.S. House of Representatives Democratic Caucus, "Who We Are," last accessed April 11, 2021, https://www.dems.gov/who-we-are.

17. U.S. Senate Republican Conference, "About the Senate Republican Conference," accessed April 11, 2021, https://www.republicans.senate.gov /public/index.cfm/about-src.

18. GovTrack.us. "2020 Report Cards," accessed April 11, 2021, https://www .govtrack.us/congress/members/report-cards/2020.

19. U.S. House of Representatives, Office of Legislative Counsel, "About: Confidentiality," accessed April 11, 2021, https://legcounsel.house.gov /about/confidentiality-and-impartiality.

20. Ibid.

21. Last accessed April 11, 2021.

22. Résumés of Congressional Activity.

23. Roger H. Davidson and Walter J. Oleszek, *Congress and Its Members*, 8th ed. (Washington, D.C.: Congressional Quarterly Press, 2002); Richard F. Fenno Jr., *Congressmen in Committees* (Boston: Little, Brown, 1973); Christopher J. Deering and Steven S. Smith, *Committees in Congress*, 3rd ed. (Washington, D.C.: Congressional Quarterly Press, 1997).

24. For the Senate, see individual committees and their subcommittees at https://www.senate.gov/committees/index.htm. For the House of Representatives, see individual committees and their subcommittees at https://www.house.gov/committees.

25. Oleszek, 150.

26. For more information about the work of the House Parliamentarian, see, last accessed April 17, 2021, https://www.house.gov/the-house-explained /officers-and-organizations/parliamentarian-of-the-house.

27. Oleszek, 172.

28. Congressional Research Service, *Senate Cloture Rule: Limitation of Debate in the Congress of the United States* and *Legislative History of Paragraph 2 of Rule XXII of the Standing Rules of the United States Senate (Cloture Rule)*, printed for the U.S. Senate Committee on Rules and Administration (Washington, D.C.: U.S. Government Printing Office, 1985).

29. Fenno, *Home Style*.

30. You can find a comprehensive database of members' electronic newsletters at http://www.dcinbox.com/. This database is the work of Professor Lindsey Cormack and several undergraduate students.

References

Alexander, Brian. *A Social Theory of Congress: Legislative Norms in the Twenty-First Century*. Lexington Books, 2021.

Angevine, Sara. "Representing All Women: An Analysis of Congress, Foreign Policy, and the Boundaries of Women's Surrogate Representation." *Political Research Quarterly* 70, no. 1 (2017): 107.

Baker, Ross K. *House and Senate*, 3d ed. New York: W.W. Norton, 2001.

Binder, Sarah. "A Primer on Self-Executing Rules." Brookings Institution Online, 2010. Last accessed March 7, 2021. **https://www.brookings .edu/blog/up-front/2010/03/17/a-primer-on-self-executing-rules/.**

Brudnick, Ida. "Salaries of Members of Congress: Recent Actions and Historical Tables." *CRS Report for Congress*. Washington, D.C.: Library of Congress, 2021.

Brudnick, Ida. "Congressional Salaries and Allowances: In Brief." *CRS Report for Congress* (Washington D.C.: Library of Congress, 2018).

Bryant, Lisa A., and Julia Marin Hellwege. "Working Mothers Represent: How Children Affect the Legislative Agenda of Women in Congress." *American Politics Research* 47, no. 3 (2019): 447–70.

Congress at Your Fingertips. Washington, D.C.: Capitol Advantage, 2002.

Congressional Research Service. Senate Cloture Rule: Limitation of Debate in the Congress of the United States and Legislative History of Paragraph 2 of Rule XXII of the Standing Rules of the United States Senate (Cloture Rule). Printed for the United States Senate Committee on Rules and Administration. Washington, D.C.: U.S. Government Printing Office, 1985.

Cox, Gary W., and Mathew D. McCubbins. Setting the Agenda: Responsible Party Government in the U.S. House of Representatives. Cambridge: Cambridge University Press, 2005.

Curry, James. *Legislating in the Dark* 3. Chicago: University of Chicago Press, 2018.

Dancey, Logan, and Geoffrey Sheagley. "Partisanship and Perceptions of Party-Line Voting in Congress." *Political Research Quarterly* 71, no. 1 (2018): 32.

Davidson, Roger H., and Walter J. Oleszek. *Congress and Its Members*, 8th ed. Washington, D.C.: Congressional Quarterly Press, 2002.

Davis, Christopher M. "The Legislative Process on the House Floor: An Introduction." *CRS Report for Congress*, 3–20. Washington, D.C.: The Library of Congress, 2019.

Deering, Christopher J., and Steven S. Smith. *Committees in Congress*, 3d ed. Washington, D.C.: Congressional Quarterly Press, 1997.

English, Ashley, Kathryn Pearson, and Dara Strolovitch. "Who Represents Me? Race, Gender, Partisan Congruence, and Representational Alternatives in a Polarized America." *Political Research Quarterly* 72, no. 4 (2019): 785–804.

Evers-Hillstrom, Karl. "State of Money in Politics: The Price of Winning is Steep." OpenSecrets.org, 2019. Last accessed March 7, 2021. **https://www.opensecrets.org/news/2019/02 /state-of-money-in-politics-the-price-of-victory-is-steep/.**

Faris, David. "Matt Gaetz and the Tyranny of the Backbencher." *The Week*, April 5, 2021. Last accessed April 10, 2021. **https://theweek.com /articles/975660/matt-gaetz-tyranny-backbencher.**

Fenno, Richard F. Jr. *Congressmen in Committees*. Boston: Little, Brown, 1973.

———. *Home Style: House Members in their Districts*. Glenview, IL: Scott Foresman, 1978.

Fowler, Linda L. "Who Runs for Congress?" *PS: Political Science & Politics* 29, no. 3 (1996). Washington, D.C.: American Political Science Association.

Galloway, George. *History of the United States House of Representatives*. Washington, D.C.: U.S. Government Printing Office, 1965.

GovTrack.us. "Statistics and Historical Comparisons," 2021. Last accessed March 6, 2021. **https://www.govtrack.us/congress/bills/statistics.**

GovTrack.us. "2020 Report Cards," 2020. Accessed April 11, 2021. **https://www.govtrack.us/congress/members/report-cards/2020.**

Hansen, Eric, and Sarah Treul. "Inexperience or Anti-Washington: Voter Preferences for Congressional Candidates." Working Paper, 2019. Last accessed April 10, 2021. **http://ehansen4.sites.luc.edu/documents /Hansen_Treul_MPSA_2019.pdf.**

Heitshusen, Valerie. "Introduction to the Legislative Process in the U.S. Congress." *CRS Report for Congress*. Washington, D.C.: The Library of Congress, 2020.

Hibbing, John R. *Congressional Careers: Contours of Life in the U.S. House of Representatives*. Chapel Hill: University of North Carolina Press, 1991.

Hudak, John. *Presidential Pork: White House Influence over the Distribution of Federal Grants*. Washington, D.C.: Brookings Institution Press, 2014.

Jacobson, Gary C., and Samuel Kernell. "Strategic Politicians" (excerpt from *Strategy and Choice in Congressional Elections*, 2d ed., 1983. In *Classics in Congressional Politics*. Herbert F. Weisberg, Eric S. Heberlig, and Lisa M. Campoli, eds. New York: Addison, Wesley, Longman, 1999.

Kazee, Thomas A., ed. *Who Runs for Congress: Ambition, Context, and Candidate Emergence*. Washington, D.C.: Congressional Quarterly Press, 1994.

Klein, Ezra. "The Most Depressing Graphic for Members of Congress." *Washington Post*, January 14, 2013. Last accessed March 6, 2021. **https://www.washingtonpost.com/news/wonk/wp/2013/01 /14/the-most-depressing-graphic-for-members-of-congress/.**

Krutz, Glen S. *Hitching a Ride: Omnibus Legislating in the U.S. Congress.* Columbus: Ohio State University Press, 2001.

Lee, Frances E. "Agreeing to Disagree: Agenda Content and Senate Partisanship, 1981–2004." *Legislative Studies Quarterly* 33, no. 2 (2008): 199–222.

Lee, Frances E., and Bruce I. Oppenheimer. *Sizing Up The Senate: The Unequal Consequences of Equal Representation.* Chicago: University of Chicago Press, 1999.

Lewis, Jan Ellen. "What Happened to the Three-Fifths Clause: The Relationship between Women and Slaves in Constitutional Thought, 1787–1866." *Journal of the Early Republic* 37, no. 1, (2017): 1–46.

Manning, Jennifer. "Membership of the 117th Congress: A Profile." *CRS Report for Congress.* March 17, 2021, 1. Washington, D.C.: Congressional Research Service.

Matthews, Donald. *U.S. Senators and Their World.* New York: W.W. Norton, 1973.

Mayhew, David. *Congress: The Electoral Connection.* New Haven, CT: Yale University Press, 1974.

Minta, Michael D., and Nadia E. Brown. "Intersecting Interests: Gender, Race, and Congressional Attention to Women's Issues," *Du Bois Review* 11, no. 2 (2014): 254.

Mulvihill, Mary E., Paul Rundquist, Judy Schneider, and Lorraine H. Tong. "House and Senate Rules of Procedure: A Comparison." *CRS Report for Congress*, April 7, 1999. Washington, D.C.: Library of Congress.

Nelson, Janai. "Counting Change: Ensuring an Inclusive Census for Communities of Color." *Columbia Law Review* 119, no. 5, (2019): 1399–1448.

Office of Legislative Counsel, United States House of Representatives. "About HOLC," 2002. Accessed December 13, 2002. **http://legcoun.house.gov/about.html.**

Oleszek, Walter J. *Congressional Procedures and the Policy Process*, 4th ed. Washington, D.C.: Congressional Quarterly Press, 2001.

"Outrageous Bills." *The Economist* 409, no. 8863 (November 23, 2013): 32.

Rackey, John D., and Lauren C. Bell. "The Incredible Shrinking Witness List: Information Loss in Congress." Unpublished manuscript, 2021.

Riotta, Chris. "GOP Aims to Kill Obamacare Yet Again After Failing 70 Times." *Newsweek* (online), 2017. Last accessed March 7, 2021. **https://www.newsweek.com/gop-health-care-bill-repeal-and-replace-70-failed-attempts-.**

Salisbury, Robert H., and Kenneth A. Shepsle. "Congressman as Enterprise." *Legislative Studies Quarterly* 6 (1981): 559–76.

Schmitt, Carly, and Hanna K. Brant. "Gender, Ambition, and Legislative Behavior in the United States House." *Journal of Women, Politics & Policy* 40, no. 2 (2019): 286–308.

Shogan, Colleen J. "Blackberries, Tweets, and YouTube: Technology and the Future of Communicating with Congress." *PS: Political Science and Politics* 43, no. 2 (2010): 231–33.

Shutt, Jennifer. "House Appropriators Officially Bring Back Earmarks, Ending Ban." RollCall.com, 2021. Last accessed March 6, 2021. **https://www.rollcall.com/2021/02/26/house-appropriators-to-cap-earmarks-at-1-percent-of-topline/.**

Sinclair, Barbara. *Unorthodox Lawmaking: New Legislative Processes in the U.S. Congress*, 5th ed. Washington, D.C.: Congressional Quarterly Press, 2016.

Standing Rules of the Senate. Washington, D.C.: U.S. Government Printing Office, 1990.

————. Washington, D.C.: U.S. Government Printing Office, 2000.

U.S. Census Bureau. "New York Congressional District 14—Representative Alexandria Ocasio-Cortez," 2019. Last accessed March 6, 2021. **https://www2.census.gov/geo/maps/cong_dist/cd116/cd_based /ST36/CD116_NY14.pdf.**

United States House of Representatives Democratic Caucus, "Who We Are," 2021. Last accessed April 11, 2021. **https://www.dems.gov /who-we-are.**

United States House of Representatives, Office of Legislative Counsel. "About: Confidentiality," 2021. Accessed April 11, 2021. **https://legcounsel .house.gov/about/confidentiality-and-impartiality.**

United States Senate Republican Conference. "About the Senate Republican Conference," 2021. Accessed April 11, 2021. **https://www.republicans .senate.gov/public/index.cfm/about-src.**

Vesoulis, Abby. "'He's Saying One Thing and Then He's Doing Another.' Rep. Madison Cawthorn Peddles a Different Kind of Trumpism in a Post-Trump World," *Time*, 2021. Last accessed March 7, 2021. **https://time .com/5931815/madison-cawthorn-post-trump/.**

Williams, Krissah. "Long Hours, Low Pay: The Thrill of It All: Job Seekers to Converge on Capitol Hill, Compete to Join Congressional Staffs." *Washington Post*, December 29, 2002, p. K1.

Witko, Christopher, Jana Morgan, Nathan J. Kelly, and Peter K. Enns. *Hijacking the Agenda: Economic Power and Political Influence*. New York: Russell Sage Foundation, 2021.

Wolfensberger, Donald. "House Rules Data," 2021, available from the Bipartisan Policy Center online. Accessed March 5, 2021. **https://bipartisanpolicy.org/report/house-rules-data/.**

Young, James Sterling. *The Washington Community 1800–1828*. New Haven, CT: Yale University Press, 1966.

Appendix I
Sample Bills/Resolutions*

Introduced in House (12/17/2020)
116th CONGRESS
2d Session
H. R. 9020

To direct the Secretary of Veterans Affairs to expedite the processing of claims for disability compensation by veterans affected by major disasters.

IN THE HOUSE OF REPRESENTATIVES
December 17, 2020

Mr. **Panetta** (for himself, Mr. **Higgins** of Louisiana, Miss **Rice** of New York, Mrs. **Axne**, Mr. **Steube**, and Ms. **Sherrill**) introduced the following bill; which was referred to the Committee on Veterans' Affairs

---

A BILL

To direct the Secretary of Veterans Affairs to expedite the processing of claims for disability compensation by veterans affected by major disasters.

Be it enacted by the Senate and House of Representatives of the United States of America in Congress assembled,

SECTION 1. SHORT TITLE.

This Act may be cited as the "Priority Response for Veterans Impacted by Disasters and Emergencies Act" or the "PROVIDE Act".

---

*The sample bills and resolutions in this appendix, as well as thousands of others, can be located using the Congress's official Web site, https://congress.gov.

SEC. 2. FINDINGS.

Congress finds the following:

(1) The Department of Veterans Affairs sets forth criteria for priority processing of veterans' disability claims by the Department.

(2) Such criteria include veterans affected by extreme financial hardship, homelessness, terminal illness, and participants in the Department's Fully Developed Claim program.

(3) Currently there is no process in place to prioritize the disability claims of veterans affected by major disasters such as fires and floods.

(4) Priority claims processing for veterans affected by major disasters will significantly help such veterans begin rebuilding their lives.

SEC. 3. PRIORITY CLAIMS PROCESSING IN THE EVENT OF A MAJOR DISASTER.

(a) In General.—The Secretary shall prescribe regulations setting forth criteria for priority processing of a claim for compensation under chapter 11 of title 38, United States Code. Individuals whose claim shall be eligible for such priority processing shall include—

(1) veterans affected by extreme financial hardship;

(2) veterans affected by homelessness;

(3) veterans diagnosed with a terminal illness;

(4) participants in the Department of Veterans Affairs Fully Developed Claim program; and

(5) veterans who live in an area for which the President has declared a major disaster under section 401 of the Robert T. Stafford Disaster Relief and Emergency Assistance Act (42 U.S.C. 5170).

(b) Special Considerations For Claims Processing In The Event Of A Major Disaster.—The Secretary shall prescribe additional regulations relating only to subsection (a)(5). Such additional regulations include—

(1) establishing flexible evidence requirements for veterans unable to meet the ordinary evidence requirements for such a claim due to a major disaster; and

(2) establishing a flexible filing deadline for such a claim.

(c) Notice To Veterans Of Eligibility For Priority Claims Processing.—Not later than 60 days after the date of enactment of this Act, the Secretary shall post a permanent notice to veterans on the Department of Veterans Affairs website of the categories of eligibility for priority processing of such claims, including the changes to such categories made pursuant to subsection (a).

★★★

Introduced in House (03/19/2021)
117th CONGRESS
1st Session

H. J. RES. 32

Proposing a balanced budget amendment to the Constitution of the United States.

IN THE HOUSE OF REPRESENTATIVES
March 19, 2021

Mr. **Obernolte** submitted the following joint resolution; which was referred to the Committee on the Judiciary

---

JOINT RESOLUTION

Proposing a balanced budget amendment to the Constitution of the United States.

Resolved by the Senate and House of Representatives of the United States of America in Congress assembled (two-thirds of each House concurring therein), That the following article is proposed as an amendment to the Constitution of the United States, which shall be valid to all intents and purposes as part of the Constitution when ratified by the legislatures of three-fourths of the several States within seven years after the date of its submission for ratification:

"Article —

"Section 1. Total outlays for any fiscal year shall not exceed total receipts for that fiscal year, unless two-thirds of the whole number of each House of Congress shall provide by law for a specific excess of outlays over receipts by a rollcall vote.

"Section 2. Prior to each fiscal year, the President shall transmit to the Congress a proposed budget for the United States Government for that fiscal year in which total outlays do not exceed total receipts.

"Section 3. The Congress shall enforce and implement this article by appropriate legislation, which may rely on estimates of outlays and receipts.

"Section 4. Total receipts shall include all receipts of the United States Government except those derived from borrowing. Total outlays shall include all outlays of the United States Government except for those for repayment of debt principal.

"Section 5. This article shall take effect beginning with the fifth fiscal year beginning after its ratification."

★★

Introduced in House (03/26/2021)
117th CONGRESS
1st Session

H. CON. RES. 25

Encouraging the Architect of the Capitol to transition to the exclusive use of electricity derived from renewable energy sources to power the United States Capitol Complex by 2032.

IN THE HOUSE OF REPRESENTATIVES
March 26, 2021

Mr. **Neguse** (for himself, Ms. **Norton**, and Mr. **Huffman**) submitted the following concurrent resolution; which was referred to the Committee on Transportation and Infrastructure

---

CONCURRENT RESOLUTION

Encouraging the Architect of the Capitol to transition to the exclusive use of electricity derived from renewable energy sources to power the United States Capitol Complex by 2032.

Whereas according to the 2018 National Climate Assessment, without substantial and sustained global mitigation and regional adaption efforts, climate change is expected to cause growing losses to American infrastructure and property and impede the rate of economic growth over this century;

Whereas according to the 2018 Intergovernmental Panel on Climate Change (IPCC) Special Report on Global Warming of 1.5° Celsius, to avoid the most devastating impacts of climate change, the world must limit the warming of the global average temperature to 1.5° Celsius above preindustrial levels;

Whereas according to the IPCC, reaching and sustaining net zero global anthropogenic carbon dioxide emissions is necessary for halting anthropogenic global warming;

Whereas according to the IPCC, in order to limit global warming to 1.5° Celsius above preindustrial levels, the world must achieve carbon neutrality by 2050, which will require rapid, dramatic changes in how governments, industries, and societies function;

Whereas the IPCC has reported that in comparison to global warming of 1.5° Celsius, global warming of 2° Celsius will result in a greater number of severe heat waves, more extreme storms, increased poverty, and the degradation of critical ecosystems;

Whereas climate change impacts will be felt disproportionately by communities of color and low-income communities;

Whereas to address the urgent need to limit global warming to 1.5° Celsius, the IPCC has recommended increasing installation of renewable energy systems, with a goal of such systems generating 70 to 80 percent of global electricity by 2050;

Whereas investing in the clean energy economy, with strong labor and procurement standards, will create quality jobs;

Whereas according to the National Oceanic and Atmospheric Administration, 2020 was the warmest year on record globally;

Whereas the world's cities occupy 2 percent of global land mass, but are responsible for up to 70 percent of harmful greenhouse gas emissions;

Whereas more than 350 mayors in the United States have adopted the Paris Agreement goals for their cities, including Washington, DC;

Whereas in the fight against climate change, cities and counties have become important leaders because of their role as laboratories, incubators, and implementers of climate solutions;

Whereas, on January 18, 2019, District of Columbia Mayor Muriel Bowser signed the CleanEnergy DC Omnibus Amendment Act of 2018, which mandates that, by 2032, 100 percent of the electricity sold at retail in the District be derived from renewable energy sources, and also includes an ambitious building performance standard; and

Whereas it is critical that Congress leads by example for American cities, communities, and people, by committing to renewable energy to combat climate change: Now, therefore, be it

Resolved by the House of Representatives (the Senate concurring),

SECTION 1. ENCOURAGING TRANSITION TO EXCLUSIVE USE OF ELECTRICITY DERIVED FROM RENEWABLE ENERGY SOURCES FOR THE UNITED STATES CAPITOL COMPLEX.

(a) Transition.—In order to address climate change, and in keeping with the recommendations of Intergovernmental Panel on Climate Change and consistent with the Building Energy Performance Standard Program of the District of Columbia, Congress encourages the Architect of the Capitol to transition to the exclusive use of electricity derived from renewable energy sources to power the United States Capitol Complex by 2032.

(b) Definition.—In this section, the term "United States Capitol Complex" means the Capitol buildings (as defined in section 5101 of title 40, United States Code) and the United States Capitol Grounds (as described in section 5102 of such title).

★★

Introduced in House (03/01/2021)
117th CONGRESS
1st Session

H. RES. 181

Amending the Rules of the House of Representatives to prohibit Members of the House from serving on the boards of for-profit entities.

IN THE HOUSE OF REPRESENTATIVES
March 1, 2021

Ms. **Craig** submitted the following resolution; which was referred to the Committee on Ethics

---

RESOLUTION

Amending the Rules of the House of Representatives to prohibit Members of the House from serving on the boards of for-profit entities.

Resolved,

SECTION 1. SHORT TITLE.

This resolution may be cited as the "Restoring Integrity in Democracy Resolution."

SEC. 2. PROHIBITING MEMBERS OF THE HOUSE OF REPRESENTATIVES FROM SERVING ON BOARDS OF FOR-PROFIT ENTITIES.

Rule XXIII of the Rules of the House of Representatives is amended—

(1) by redesignating clauses 19 through 22 as clauses 20 through 23, respectively; and

(2) by inserting after clause 18 the following new clause:

"19. A Member, Delegate, or Resident Commissioner may not serve on the board of directors of any for-profit entity."

★★★

Appendix II
Sample Dear Colleague Letters*

November 10, 2020

Dear Colleague:

One of the biggest winners of the 2020 election was cannabis reform. Americans in five very different states voted overwhelmingly to liberalize their cannabis policies, and it is clearer than ever that the American people are demanding a change to outdated cannabis laws. There's no question: cannabis prohibition will end soon. We should lead the way by passing H.R.3884 - Marijuana Opportunity Reinvestment and Expungement (MORE) Act.

Last week's results reaffirm the strong bipartisan support to reform our failed cannabis prohibition. Even in states where Republicans easily swept elections, like in Mississippi and South Dakota, cannabis-related ballot measures passed with strong support. The success in Arizona, Montana, Mississippi, New Jersey, and South Dakota means that cannabis will be legal for adult use in 15 states and medical use in 36 states. More than 109 million people will live in states where cannabis is legal for adults to use, that is more than one in three Americans. In total, almost 99% of Americans will live in states with some form of legal cannabis. We cannot ignore the will of the people any longer.

This comes as no surprise—national support for federal cannabis legalization is at an all-time high, and trends show that support will continue to grow. Polling from the Pew Research Center shows that 67% of registered voters think "the use of cannabis should be made legal," and the Center for American Progress found that 73% support expunging the records of those previously convicted of cannabis-related offenses. This finding is confirmed by the fact that in the last three elections, 16 of the 18 pro-cannabis reform ballot initiatives were successful—even in places like Utah and Mississippi.

---

*Common Cause makes available a searchable database of Dear Colleague letters at http://dearcolleague.wpengine.com/. Some members of Congress make Dear Colleague letters available on their own websites at https://www.house.gov and https://www.senate.gov. The Dear Colleague letters sampled here are taken verbatim from the sources indicated. They have been edited only to remove the names of specific congressional staff members when necessary

This past election further demonstrated that cannabis reform is popular, non-partisan, and the just thing to do as states have also made clear their commitment to restorative justice. Montana, which ranks first in the country for having the largest racial disparities for cannabis arrests will allow an individual currently serving a sentence for a prior low-level cannabis offense to apply for resentencing or an expungement of the conviction.

The recent success of cannabis reform in states around the country should give us a new sense of urgency to ensure Congress catches up with the American people. This is a critical issue of racial justice, and the failed war on drugs has devastated communities of color, especially Black and Brown communities. We can no longer ignore our duty to repair the damage that this harmful form of systemic racism has done.

The House was poised to vote on the MORE Act, the most comprehensive federal cannabis reform legislation we've ever seen, back in September. As the House kept our focus on providing struggling Americans with relief from COVID-19, we received commitment from our Caucus leadership that Congress would take steps to end the failed war on drugs by voting on the MORE Act before the year was over.

We have an opportunity and duty to correct course now. As we head into the lame-duck session, we must remember the promise we made to the American people to pass the MORE Act.

Thank you for your urgency.

Courage,

Earl Blumenauer   Barbara Lee
House Cannabis Caucus Co-Chair   House Cannabis Caucus Co-Chair

★★★

Source: accessed April 11, 2021,

https://blumenauer.house.gov/sites/blumenauer.house.gov/files/2020
-11-10%20Caucus%20DC%20from%20cannabis%20co-chairs%20on%20
MORE%20Act%20committment%202.pdf.

June 16, 2020

Dear Colleague:

We write in strong support of the Justice in Policing Act of 2020 (H.R. 7120) and urge you to cosponsor and vote in favor of the bill when it comes to the floor.

The murders of George Floyd, Breonna Taylor, Ahmaud Arbery, and countless other Black Americans make clear that policing in the United States must change. These traumatic experiences are the latest public illustration of the violence inflicted on Black communities each day by the very people and institutions that should be there to protect them. It is due time that Congress provide real, equitable reforms that ensure officers empathize with and understand the communities they serve.

The growing divide between our men and women in blue and the public they are sworn to protect is unhealthy for democracy, and unhealthy for public safety. While not universal, many law enforcement leaders and rank and file officers recognize the gravity of this moment. If trust between communities of color and those sworn to protect them is not achieved now, it may be irreparably broken.

The Justice in Policing Act provides several necessary reforms that aim to rebuild trust between law enforcement officers and the communities they serve and prevent needless and tragic deaths from occurring in the future. If enacted, this legislation would achieve transformative, structural change to combat the pattern of police brutality and racial injustice by outlawing racial profiling, mandating de-escalation training, banning chokeholds and other excessively violent techniques, stanching the flow of military equipment onto our street corners, and bringing transparency and accountability to policing.

The brutal deaths of Mr. Floyd, Ms. Taylor, and of Tamir Rice, Eric Garner, and Philando Castile, among many other Black Americans shows something is badly broken and urgent cultural and structural change in policing is needed. We must heed the call of the millions rallying, protesting, and crying out for justice and follow through on reforms that improve policing and make our country safer.

We thank the sponsors of the *Justice in Policing Act* for their leadership on this critical legislation. We urge you all to cosponsor and vote in favor of this bill to bring real, structural reform to policing in our country and make unmistakably clear that Black Lives Matter.

Sincerely,

Bill Pascrell, Jr.	Val B. Demings	Tom O'Halleran
Member of Congress	Member of Congress	Member of Congress

★★★

Source: accessed April 11, 2021, https://pascrell.house.gov/news /documentsingle.aspx?DocumentID=4343.

Appendix III
Getting a Job or Internship in the Congress

Many students in political science hope one day to work on Capitol Hill. As you know, congressional staff serves many important functions. Staff members at the entry levels ensure the smooth operation of the office. They transact much of the routine business and the constituency service that is the lifeblood of members' work and reelection campaigns. Staff members also monitor pending legislation, and many of them write legislation, determine legislative strategy, and even represent their elected bosses at important governmental functions. For these reasons, working on the Hill is exciting and fast-paced; however, it can also be difficult work to find right out of college, in large part because Hill jobs often require previous experience in the form of an internship and/or a prior relationship with the person doing the hiring. In other words, getting a job on Capitol Hill requires good networking skills and—often—prior experience. For that reason, it's important to try to get experience before graduation in the form of an internship or summer job with a member's office. Internships can serve another important function as well: During the course of your internship on Capitol Hill, you might discover that you are simply not going to enjoy the high-pressure, fast-paced demands of working in the U.S. Congress. It is much better to realize that before you have signed a long-term lease and moved to D.C.!

If you are serious about getting an internship on the Hill, you will need to plan ahead. There are two main ways of tracking down an internship. The first is to pound the pavement, which means that you should start by contacting anyone you know who has a connection to Capitol Hill—a friend with an entry-level position, an uncle who lobbies on the Hill, or a neighbor who used to work for a senator, for example, could each likely put you in touch with someone in a position to offer you a job or internship. A lot of students worry about doing this. They don't want to get a job simply based on their connections, or they worry that asking a friend to talk to someone in her office about job openings will cause the chief of staff to think they are annoying. Wrong! Anyone who has ever worked on Capitol Hill will tell you that networking is absolutely essential to getting a job or internship—and that the more you network, the better chance you'll have of finding a position. Although it certainly varies from office to office, the average tenure in entry level roles is somewhere between six months and one year before those staff members are promoted to more senior roles. That means that offices are always looking for talented people to hire at the entry level.

Pounding the pavement also means calling congressional offices, consulting their websites, and making "cold calls" to offices that may or may not be accepting internship applications. Most offices begin accepting applications for summer interns around the first of the year—by March, nearly all offices have accepted all the interns they plan to accept for the summer. In some cases, members' offices will even have accepted interns for the following summer. So, the bottom line is that the serious intern candidate has to be organized well in advance of the date he or she wishes to start working.

The second method of finding an internship—which is frequently more costly, but generally offers a better chance of finding an internship—is to work through an established, credit-bearing Washington semester or Washington internship program. Many institutions have their own semester- or summer-long D.C. internship programs; there are also several well-established internship programs open to students from any institution. Two are noted later in the section "Semester-Long Internship Programs."

With most Hill internships, do not expect to be paid for your efforts. Although a good intern is invaluable to a member of Congress and his or her congressional staff, there are literally thousands of prospective interns from whom members can choose. Over the last several years, more offices have begun to offer some remuneration to student interns—sometimes in the form of a stipend or transportation voucher. Still, paid internships are not yet the norm on Capitol Hill and there remain relatively few internship opportunities that will provide regular compensation. Some offices will work with you to try to help you get course credit for the work you put in, but others won't. (That doesn't mean that your own institution doesn't have a provision to allow you to get credit—and you should look into that any time you decide to do an internship.)

Much of this same advice applies to the person who is looking for a job on the Hill. However, in the case of bona fide job openings, it does not make sense to apply for a job far in advance of when you will be available to start. It is standard for most staff members to give two weeks' notice that they are leaving. Give or take a day, this frequently means that the office wants someone to be able to start in two weeks or less. When you see a job listing, you should apply *as quickly as possible.* You should also be certain to follow the instructions in the advertisement. If the ad says "no phone calls," then don't call. If the ad says to include a writing sample, then include a writing sample. Brief research or reaction papers or published articles (such as in a campus newspaper or journal of student writing) typically make fine writing samples.

Sometimes, the advertisement won't specify the name of the member of Congress who is hiring; instead, it will simply say something to the effect of "Progressive northeastern Democratic senator seeks . . . ." This can be disconcerting, but it's fairly common. The reason these advertisements sometimes do not list the member's name is that some members have reputations—good or bad—that might make people more or less likely to apply for the position. For example, an advertisement that says "Conservative Southern Republican Senator seeks . . . ." would be more likely to yield applicants who are sincere in their ideological beliefs, whereas "Senator Tommy Tuberville seeks . . . ." might yield a whole host of applicants who are neither interested in nor qualified for the position, but who simply want to work for a senator who was previously a decorated college football coach at Auburn University.

The types of jobs that you will likely be qualified for as a recent college graduate (with or without prior internship experience) have titles such as "staff assistant," "legislative correspondent," or "constituency relations specialist." These are considered entry level, and are a good way to get your foot in the door on the Hill. Keep in mind, however, that these jobs frequently have starting salaries in the mid- to high-$20,000 range, so most entry-level staff must share housing with others or live with family in the area in order to afford to live close to work.

Finally, whether you are applying for a job or an internship, you will want to be certain to approach offices in a professional manner. I've already explained that you should follow the directions listed in the position advertisement. In addition, you should dress appropriately for an interview. In fact, you should dress professionally even if all you are doing is dropping off resumes. You never know whom you might encounter when you walk through a congressional office's front door. In addition, never assume that the person sitting behind the desk is an intern—for all you know, it could be the office's chief of staff, even if he or she looks young, is dressed casually, and is sitting at the front desk. When I worked on the Hill, the chief counsel of a Senate Judiciary Committee subcommittee told me a story: She always took her interns with her to meetings, and in one case, the intern happened to be a man in his mid-thirties. At a meeting with staff members from the White House Office of Legislative Affairs, the White House staffer walked in, looked at the two of them, and assumed that the intern (because he was older and male) was the chief counsel. The White House staff member barely glanced at the *real* chief counsel, who was actually responsible for making the decisions that the White House cared about. Needless to say, the White House staffer didn't get what he asked for during the meeting. The moral of the story, of course, is: Don't make assumptions; treat everyone courteously and with respect.

The *Washington Post* offers the following additional suggestions about interviewing:

1. Do your homework. Be prepared and research the member of Congress or the committees that you're approaching.

2. Know your politics. It's important to know who represents your district, who your senators are, what happened in recent political campaigns, and what issues are important to your region and state.

3. Be open to a variety of positions and opportunities. A key goal is getting a foot in the door, so look at committees, congressional research organizations, and internships.

4. Don't burn bridges during your job search. You'll be amazed who's up and down in one week in Washington.[1]*

There are many, many opportunities to find internships and jobs on the Hill. It does take time and effort, however, and to that end, I've compiled a list of sources and resources that you might find helpful as you think about your future career plans. Some of these resources are in the form of job lines and

---

*Krissah Williams, "Long Hours, Low Pay: The Thrill of It All: Job Seekers to Converge on Capitol Hill, Compete to Join Congressional Staffs," *Washington Post*, December 29, 2002, p. K1.

government information hotlines. Others provide important information about how members' offices function. Not all of these are links for internships in the Congress itself; many government offices provide internships that are related to the Congress. Moreover, finding an internship or a job in the Congress can be difficult, so gaining experience through other Capitol Hill and government positions can be an excellent way to build your resume toward finding that job in the U.S. Congress.

Employment Opportunities

Administrative Office of the U.S. Courts

Thurgood Marshall Building

Washington, D.C. 20544

Employment Opportunities List:

https://www.uscourts.gov/careers

Office of Personnel Management (Executive Branch Positions)

https://opm.usajobs.gov/

https://www.usajobs.gov/help/working-in-government/unique-hiring-paths/students/

United States Department of Labor

https://www.apprenticeship.gov/

U.S. House of Representatives

House Employment Office

H2-102 Ford House Office Building

Washington, D.C. 20515

Employment Office webpage: https://www.house.gov/employment.

U.S. Senate

116 Hart Senate Office Building

Washington, D.C. 20510

Senate Employment Bulletin: www.senate.gov/employment.

U.S. Supreme Court

Internship information: https://www.supremecourt.gov/jobs/internship/internshipprogram.aspx.

Semester-Long Internship Programs

The Washington Center

2301 M Street NW, Fifth Floor

Washington, D.C. 20037

http://www.twc.edu

American University's Washington Semester Program
4400 Massachusetts Avenue NW
Washington, D.C. 20016-8083
Toll-Free: 800-424-2600
Local: 202-895-4900
https://www.american.edu/spexs/washingtonsemester/
washsem@american.edu

Political Parties

Republican National Committee (RNC)
310 First Street SE
Washington, D.C. 20003
202-863-8500
https://www.gop.com/

Democratic National Committee (DNC)
430 South Capitol Street SE
Washington, D.C. 20003
202-863-8000
http://www.democrats.org

Dedicated DC Job/Internship Sites and Newspaper Classified Advertisements

These classified listings include jobs not only inside the Congress but also in lobbying firms that work with the Congress.

Roll Call
(Capitol Hill newspaper)
Online at: https://www.rcjobs.com/

The Hill
(Capitol Hill newspaper—more conservative than *Roll Call*)
Online at: https://thehill.com/resources/classifieds/employer

The Washington Post
(major Washington, D.C., newspaper)
Online at https://jobs.washingtonpost.com

Traverse Jobs
([Small] fee-for-service Washington, D.C., employment service)
Online at: https://www.traversejobs.com/.

Other Opportunities to Get Involved in Congress

Working or interning for a member of Congress or related agency is not the only way to get involved with the institution. Even short-term visitors to Washington, D.C., can join tours of the Capitol building and gardens. House and Senate offices can set up Capitol tours for you by contacting them directly, or tours can be arranged, including specialty tours, through the Capitol Visitor's Center. (For reservations through the Capitol Visitors' Center, go to: https://www.visitthecapitol.gov/plan-visit/book-tour-capitol.) Members and Senators can also arrange for gallery passes that allow you to sit in either the House or Senate galleries (or both!) to watch debate taking place when Congress is in session. In addition to touring and visiting the galleries, nearly all congressional hearings are open to the public on a first-come, first-served basis. Congress's official website, Congress.gov, tracks all scheduled House and Senate hearings at https://www.congress.gov/committee-schedule.

Finally, many organized interests will hold "lobby days" on Capitol Hill. These are days when the organization's members will meet in Washington, D.C., for one or more days of scheduled events, including meetings or briefings with members of Congress. If you are a member of an organization or have a deep interest in a particular set of issues, getting involved with lobby day activities is a good way to network with other like-minded individuals and to be a part of the legislative process.

Index